RETRIEVAL-BASED LEARNING

CONNOR WHITELEY

No part of this book may be reproduced in any form or by any electronic or mechanical means. Including information storage, and retrieval systems, without written permission from the author except for the use of brief quotations in a book review.

This book is NOT legal, professional, medical, financial or any type of official advice.

Any questions about the book, rights licensing, or to contact the author, please email connorwhiteley@connorwhiteley.net

Copyright © 2024 CONNOR WHITELEY

All rights reserved.

DEDICATION
Thank you to all my readers without you I couldn't do what I love.

INTRODUCTION

This is definitely a book that I never ever would have imagined I would ever write, because cognitive psychology isn't really my area of interest. I am much more of a clinical psychology type of man. Yet that's why this book on the psychology of learning is really interesting, different and it is far from a boring, dull textbook.

We all know that learning is critical in everyday life. We know that we need to learn how to do things, we need to learn for school and we need to learn for the sake of our careers.

Leading us to the question about what is the most effective way to learn?

That's where Retrieval-Based Learning comes in, because this is a great, effective, fascinating form of learning that gets a learner to actively recall the information they learn so they are more likely to remember it later on when tested.

Therefore, for my Final Year Project in the

2022/2023 academic year, I research Retrieval-Based Learning and wrote a dissertation on it, and because the topic was really fun and interesting I wanted to share it all with you.

And if you're a long-term reader of mine then you know that another reason why I wanted to do this book was so I could explain the fun, troubles and funny moments that happened along the way.

We all know that when it comes to research there is a lot more blood, sweat and tears that goes into it, and academic writing doesn't allow us to explain the behind-the-scenes aspects that always goes on. That's something else I write about in this book to help the topic come alive and make it a lot more interesting.

That's why so we can explore this brilliant topic in a way that makes sense, gives you all the information you need and you can see what we did in the research. You'll be following the structure of my project and I'll confess that considering I am really interested in clinical psychology and I don't really care about cognitive psychology. This was a great project to do because I learnt a lot, met a lot of great people and the results were shocking.

In a good way.

Why Buy This Book?

Like all of my books, this is written for university psychology students and psychology professionals that want to learn more about psychology. In this case, I admit this book is written more towards psychology students so they can understand how a

Final Year Project works, the sort of interesting challenges you can expect and you can learn about cognitive psychology at the same time.

Also, like all of my other books, this is always written in an engaging, easy-to-understand way that not only delivers fact-based, high-quality information in a fun way that actually makes you want to read it, but the material comes alive.

Something that is almost non-existent in psychology textbooks.

Overall, if you want to learn more about the psychology of learning, what happens on a Final Year Project/ undergraduate Dissertation or you just want to read more about cognitive psychology and the psychology student life. Then you will love this book.

Who Am I?

Personally, I always love to know who the author is of the nonfiction I read so I know the information is coming from a good source. In case you're like me, I'm Connor Whiteley, the internationally bestselling author of over 40 psychology books.

In addition, I am the host of *The Psychology World Podcast,* a weekly show exploring a new psychology topic each week and delivering the latest psychology news. Available on all major podcast apps and YouTube.

Finally, I am a psychology graduate studying a Clinical Psychology Masters at the University of Kent, England.

So now we know more about each other, let's

dive into the great topic of Retrieval-based Learning.

WHAT IS RETRIEVAL-BASED LEARNING?

Kicking off this book and as I mentioned in the introduction, we're going to be following the structure of my dissertation and I'm going to introduce you to this brilliant and really interesting topic before explaining more about the experiment itself.

Therefore, we can probably know, learning is critical in everyday life from learning how to ride a bike to how to revise effectively for exams to how to drive a car, learning is everywhere, and we also know that learning requires a lot of cognitive skills including memory retrieval as retrieval enhances learning (Roediger & Karpicke, 2006).

Knowing the above is important because it is this understanding of the skills behind learning that lead to the development of retrieval-based learning tasks. As well as this is where learners' re-access newly learnt stimuli by undergoing tests.

Typically, participants in a retrieval-based learning task have an initial learning phase, where learners are tested on said stimuli, next is a testing phase, where the learners are tested on this material. Also, retrieval-based learning tasks utilise various combinations of these study-test blocks. Such as, STST, STTT, etc (Pyke et al., 2021).

Whereas when a researcher decides to use a control condition, in this case learners aren't tested on the learnt material and all learners complete a final assessment to measure their overall learning, with these assessments taking place minutes (Smith et al., 2013) or months (Carpenter et al., 2009) after the previous phases. You'll see how we did this in two chapter's time.

In addition, retrieval-based learning tasks have been found in research to be beneficial for a wide range of populations, including patients (Friedman et al., 2017), children (Lipowski et al., 2014) and older adults (Coane, 2013) and retrieval-based learning reliably shows increased long-term retention of learnt stimuli compared to study-only conditions (Agarwal et al., 2008; Fazio & Marsh, 2019; Karpicke & Grimaldi, 2012; Roediger & Butler, 2011).

Personally, after learning and looking at that small introduction to retrieval-based learning, I have to admit that this type of learning is really interesting. Because something me and the girls I was working with said was that when we were first introduced to the project we weren't sure if this was going to work.

Since this literature sounds great and very, very impressive but don't all overexaggerated things? Like social priming, the research sounds amazing, for example the idea that holding a warm mug of coffee can make you more positive. It sounds fun and great but the research is beyond stupid.

That's sort of what me and my friends thought about retrieval-based learning when we first encountered it, but I promise you it really is amazing and fascinating to see in action.

Anyway, the very notion of learning via retrieval started in the early 20th century (Abbott, 1909; Gates, 1917, Spitzer, 1939) and it was Bjork's (1994) Desirable Difficulties Framework that bought the idea of difficulty and effort into the forefront of retrieval-based learning and it does nicely fit with retrieval-based learning for this reason. Due to the Framework proposes an effective way to improve long-term retention by learnt stimuli is to introduce a desirable amount of difficulty (effort) whilst learning.

Furthermore, the role of effort in retrieval-based learning can be explained by the Retrieval Effort Hypothesis (REH) which is consistent with Bjork's (1994) framework because the REH states the more difficult retrieval is, the more effort the learner requires and this increases the probability the material will be consolidated in the long-term memory and make the retrieval easier later on as supported by several studies (Carprenter & DeLosh, 2006; Karpicke & Roediger, 2007b; Pyc & Rawson, 2009).

Nonetheless, the biggest problem with this theory is that REH has been criticised for being too descriptive (Karpicke et al., 2014) and fails to explain how effort could produce memory benefits. As well as the literature agrees it remains difficult to truly compare cued recall and free recall tests because of aspects like false alarm rates and response pressure in cued recall tests (Ozubko, 2011).

What Theories And Models Explain The Effectiveness Of Retrieval-Based Learning?

In addition, this is where we get into the information that isn't covered in my project because I didn't feel like it was relevant to the actual focus of the investigation. But I want to include it in here because it helps to explain the general background to learning better.

As a result, a range of theories have been put forward over the decades to explain the effectiveness of retrieval-based learning. One such theory is the Stretch Theory (Murdock & Dufty, 1972; Norman & Wickelgren, 1969; Wickelgren & Norman, 1966) because this provides researchers with a general theoretical model for recognition memory, where the more information is recalled or "remembered" the stronger the memory trace. Leaving a physical record of the memories in the brain (Thompson, 2005) and the more this is recalled the easier the information is to recall in the future.

Moreover, another theory is the Transfer Appropriate Processing (TAP) theory and this states the initial practise test prepares the participant for the final test by eliciting a similar type of working memory processing compared to studying the material alone (Roediger & Karpicke, 2006). Consequently, the testing effect, where the performance difference between the study-only and RBL group, is greater when the task used in the initial encoding is the same as the final test. This is where the baseline and training sessions aren't similar to all the testing phases we use because we wanted to make sure the performance of the participant was down to them learning and not the Testing Effect.

Thirdly, the Bifurcation model proposed by Kornell et al. (2011) states during a retrieval-based learning condition using free or cued recall tests without corrective feedback, a split occurs in later recall tests. Successfully retrieved items on an initial test creates a stronger memory trace, compared to items that are forgotten. Therefore, creating a bifurcated item distribution where initially recalled items are more likely to be remembered later on compared to items that are forgotten.

In other words, participants are more likely to remember correct answers than wrong ones because during the training sessions the correct answers make a stronger memory trace so these are recalled later, and the wrong answers are forgotten.

What Is An Alternative Theory To REH?

Personally, I would have liked to include this theory in my project but I did understand how this didn't really add anything to the final submission. Yet I really did want to add it in this book so you can understand how learning happens according to a wide range of theories and models.

Nonetheless, you might have noticed that all the above theories and models focus on the idea of the learner having to put effort into learning and there's the idea of a physical memory trace. But are there any other ideas to explain the effectiveness of retrieval-based learning?

One alternative theory is the Cognitive Load Theory (CLT) by Sweller (1988) and Sweller et al. (1998) and this aims to explain the link between cognitive load (processing load) and how this impacts a learner's ability to manage new information and learning tasks and how this is later built into knowledge in the long-term memory.

In addition, this theory is built on three critical assumptions. Firstly, the long-term memory consists of schemas categorising information based on how it will be used (Chi et al., 1982) and has an unlimited capacity. Secondly, the working memory has limited capacity and consists of multiple semi-independent subsystems. These two assumptions form a third where learning is most effective when instructional procedures are used limiting the working memory load whilst concurrently encouraging schema formation.

In terms of research support for Cognitive Load Theory, the evidence mainly comes from studies that show the supporting effects that the theory proposes (Sweller et al., 1998). For instance, the goal-free effect, this is where learners encounter a novel problem without a schema readily available to help them, making the learners engage in a means-end Analysis (MEA), where they identify a goal state and problem state. Once they've done this, these two states require the learner to reconcile the differences between the states using a problem-solving operator (Sweller, 1988) and if no goal state is clear for the learner, they identify the problem state and apply a problem-solving operator to this problem. The theory is backed by practice as research shows in multiple experimental contexts this method reduces working memory load and increases schema construction, resulting in improved memorisation (Ayres, 1993; Bobis et al., 1994; Owen & Sweller, 1985; Vollmeyer et al., 1996).

What Is Transfer Effect?

Now that we understand a lot about learning and how retrieval-based learning works from a theoretical standpoint, let's move onto what the project actually focused on, or at least the viewpoint that I wanted to explore in depth for the sake of my dissertation.

I really wanted to focus on something known as Transfer Effect.

This is a theory that is officially called Transfer Appropriate Processing (TAP) or Transfer Effect and this is the proactive use of prior learning in a novel context (Pan & Rickard, 2018) with this brand-new context potentially referring to any situation that is somehow different to the context the learning originally took place in (McDaniel, 2007). Such as, a different test type, goal or topic (Barnett & Ceci, 2002).

In addition, this links to effort because the TAP proposes a process of spreading activation occurs during the search for answers on a test (Anderson, 1996; Collins & Loftus, 1975; Raaijmakers & Shiffrin, 1981), creating multiple retrieval cues to aid later recall. This results in the testing effect (Pan & Rickard, 2018) and Pan and Rickard (2018) believed Transfer Effects could result from the same mechanism, because semantically-related information similar to the previously learnt stimuli needs to be recalled on a transfer test.

As a result, the process of spreading activation that presumably occurs during the initial testing increases the likelihood this learnt information will be recallable as well (Carpenter, 2011; Chan, 2009; Chan, McDermott, & Roediger, 2006; Cranney, Ahn, McKinnon, Morris, & Watts, 2009) suggesting participants implicitly employ techniques to carry out learning resulting in effort likely being reduced.

On the whole, Pan and Rickard (2018) concluded test-enhanced learning could yield transfer performance substantially better than non-testing re-exposure conditions. This supports this paper's examination as our Retrieval-Based Learning task will help to provide further evidence for the efficacy of test-enhanced learning and Transfer Effects.

In other words, Transfer Effect is all about how a learner applies the learning they did in one context and transfers that learning to another similar context so they can do just as well as they did in the same similar context. As we go on through the book, you'll understand how this happens in our training sessions.

However, so far, we've only focused on behavioural theories and considering this was an EEG project, what biological theories could possibly explain learning in the brain?

WHAT ARE THE BIOLOGICAL UNDERPINNINGS OF RETRIEVAL-BASED LEARNING?

Now that we understand the behavioural theory behind this project, we need to understand how Transfer Learning could possibly happen from a biological or neurological viewpoint, because there absolutely has to be something in the brain or our biology that allows this mechanism of learning to happen.

That's why we need to look at the several biological processes that could be responsible for Transfer Effects.

What Is Long-Term Potentiation?

One reason how Transfer Effects could happen from a biological standpoint is by Long-term Potentiation (LTP) and this is the strengthening of synapses based on recent neural activation producing a long-lasting increase in information transmission between two neurons (Cooke and Bliss, 2006). This is important in learning because Long-term Potentiation underpins neuroplasticity (Bliss and Collingridge, 1993). Which relates to Transfer Effect because memories are believed to be encoded according to synaptic strength.

As a result, Long-term Potentiation is a major mechanism behind learning and memory (Bliss and Collingridge, 1993; Cooke and Bliss, 2006) possibly aiding in the process of spreading activation and creating retrieval cues for later recall as TAP proposes.

Neural Efficiency Hypothesis

I have a funny story to tell you about this theory in a moment.

A second theory explaining Transfer Effects is the Neural Efficiency Hypothesis that proposes during a cognitive task, people with higher brain activation compared to low activation will be more successful at the task (Dunst et al., 2014) suggesting performance differences are caused by differences in the efficacy of a person's neural processing (Neubauer and Fink, 2009).

Therefore, this supports Transfer Effect because it would explain neurologically why some participants are better at a task compared to others, and presumably not as able to apply learning across similar contexts when learning new stimuli.

The funny thing about this theory was that when I was looking it up, I was first introduced to the theory using the wording as something along the lines of "bright people had higher brain activation and dim people had lower brain activation…"

No kidding. That was basically the word of an official academic paper on a journal website. I was surprised to say the least and I was fairly shocked. I laughed about it and I am very happy that I changed my wording.

Why Use EEG?

One of the reasons I actually chose to work on this project is simply because it would allow me to work with EEG. I wanted to do this because neuroimaging techniques are very rare opportunities to work on and they are really interesting.

Therefore, not only did I want to broaden my research skills by learning about how to work with EEG and I learnt how painful the analysis is (more on that later on) but I wanted to take advantage of this neuroimaging research project, because I honestly doubt I will ever have the chance to work with it again.

Especially as I have no interest in going into academic research.

Additionally, in case you aren't familiar with EEG, this piece of neuroimaging technology measures neuron electrical activity in the brain (Wu et al., 2016) and depending on the type of memory being retrieved different brain areas require different neural oscillations for successful encoding (Khader et al., 2010) (just think brain waves. That's the normal way to say it). For instance, stronger alpha activity has been found in occipital-to-parietal scalp sites for subsequently remembered stimuli, and stronger theta power has been found for subsequently remembered stimuli over parietal-to-central electrodes.

This does suggest to researchers that alpha and theta oscillations (brain waves) do moderate or control successful long-term memory encoding (Khader et al., 2010) and theta activity is involved in working memory maintenance (Hsieh et al., 2014) with frontal theta oscillations playing a causal role in prioritizing working memory representations (Riddle et al., 2020).

Moreover, Nguyen et al. (2018) shows us how EEG can be used to quantify 'effort' in empirical investigations allowing this paper to empirically measure the effects of RBL on a participant's neuroactivity.

And that reference was a massive pain to find because in my project, I really, really needed to find some evidence that you can use EEG to research effort objectively, but it is a weird case of every academic "knows" it can be. But to actually find research evidence for that "fact" is very hard. Especially when no researchers outright imply or state that EEG can be used to investigate effort.

That's why in my research we wanted to investigate Transfer Effect using Electroencephalogram (EEG) to provide supporting evidence for the neural basis of transfer effects, something that just hasn't been done until now.

In addition, another large section that was deleted from my original introduction was a little bit more supporting evidence for neural activity's role in learning. Due to research shows that neural brain activity has a wide range of effects on working memory, which as we know by now is involved in learning (Reber and Kotovsky, 1997; Schuler et al., 2011).

For example, frontal midline theta is critical for cognitive controls in and acts functionally different depending on task demands (Eschmann et al., 2018), and alpha brainwaves increase significantly during memory retrieval compared to demand and attentional tasks, and increasing alpha synchronisation with memory retrieval increases good memory performance (Klimesch et al., 1993). Therefore, this suggests a decrease in alpha synchronisation always leads to a decrease in memory performance, and supporting the role of brain oscillatory activity in memory.

Also, when theta power increases during the memory encoding of words, more words are remembered later on and alpha power decreases during encoding yet did not always show significant differences in the alpha band between words remembered and not remembered (Klimesch and Doppelmayr, 1996). These human results are supported by animal studies as well, since Jutras and Buffalo (2014) demonstrated changes in medial temporal lobe activity across multiple frequency bands associated with stimulus novelty, familiarity, memory reactivation, temporal resolution, associative learning, and memory encoding provided evidence that neural oscillations could influence interactions between neurons during learning to encourage the formation of functional networks ready for later activation for consolidation or retrieval. Overall, lending supporting evidence to how transfer effects could work in the brain.

Bringing This All Together

If we bring this all together, I want to stress that the entire reason why we needed to do the research was because no academic paper until now has ever provided neurological evidence (brain wave evidence in this case) for Transfer Effect. Therefore, this is why we wanted to see how the brain reflects the amount of effort university students put into learning because of transfer effect techniques by measuring differences in EEG activity in Session 1 and Session 5.

I hypothesised that the participant's theta activity will decrease from Session 1 to Session 5. As well as I wanted to examine the participant's performance improvement over time with me predicting that despite participants learning novel stimuli in each training session, they will improve between Session 1 to Session 5, indicating transfer effects.

So now the introductory topics are all done, how did we go about doing the research?

HOW WAS THE EXPERIMENT DONE?

Now that we understand how Retrieval-Based Learning works and what we were trying to achieve with the research study, we need to look at how we actually went about doing this research.

And it was actually the research methods itself that really sold me on this project because I had always wanted to use Eeg equipment, because it is fairly rare for students to get to work on neuroimaging projects, and EEG had always sounded like a lot of fun.

Therefore, I want to explain the methods section, because it is interesting and there are some funny stories that happened along the way.

How Did We Get Participants?

I'll share a few funny stories in a moment but to know how many participants we needed for the study we used G*Power 3.1.9.7 to run a priori (before) power analysis so we understood how many participants we would need to get to create a powerful study.

That meant we needed about 50 participants, and we got these using volunteer sampling through the university's Research Participation Scheme that as you can imagine is a compulsory requirement of all psychology degrees in the UK (and I think everywhere) so they can understand and contribute to research.

We only wanted to use students that were aged between 19 and 32 with a mean age of 20 years old and 43 of these participants were female. This isn't surprising to be honest given how female-heavy psychology degrees are.

In addition, the exclusion criteria is rather interesting because you cannot use EEG equipment on certain people, like people with afros because it negatively impacts how the electrodes touch the scalp.

Other exclusion criterion for the study included any previous knowledge of any logographic language, the person being left-handed, having learning difficulties, like dyslexia and being outside of the age range. Yet participant nationality and ethnicity demographics weren't collected. As well as, you can probably imagine that we naturally had to compensate students for their time so they got course credits and £10.

Now the funny story about participants is twofold. Firstly, if you ever do psychology research, just hope beyond hope that you get your participants near the start of the term. Since we found out (and this happens every year according to my supervisor) that the good engaged students do their credits straight away. Whereas the students that cannot be used don't, they leave their credits towards the end and that is when you have your no-shows and nightmare participants.

It was a very relaxed final few weeks of term

because we simply had so many dropouts. It was annoying as hell but it's life.

Secondly, we did have a nightmare when it came to the EEG results because it turned out over the summer before my Final Year Project started, someone had actually gone into the EEG lab, messed around with the cables and the EEG amplifier (a very important piece of software) was not plugged into the computer properly.

Meaning the first two weeks of EEG data was never recorded. We thought we were doing so well and then yeah, it turns out we were missing people's data.

A funny if not tragic start to the year.

How Was The Study Designed?

I know some of you will be wanting to know the design details of the study so it is a quasi-experimental study using a mixed factorial design, with one ratio and two categorical independent variables (IVs), these were: Performance, Session, and Block.

Additionally, the dependent variables (DVs) for the study were Successful Retrievals, Response Latency, Untimed Cued-Recall Score, and Theta Power, with a controlled variable being the day on which each session occurred.

On a personal note, I will confess that doing this research did make me appreciate quasi-research a little more. Since there are some things in life, some things in psychology and some topics in the literature that you simply cannot create a "true" research study for.

I mean a "real" experiment is when you have your independent variable then you change something leading to your dependent variable and you control for all other variables. As you can see with any study we weren't really changing anything, we gave participants a task but we didn't change a variable.

Before this study I thought that was "bad" or at least not ideal research, but now I realise it was the best way to do it at this moment in time.

How Was The Study Done?

I know, I know normally the material section of the methods comes next but this is my book and I realised that the material section made no sense without this part first.

And come on, how a study is actually done is a lot more interesting than some silly materials.

General Procedure

As a result, I really liked that our study was a long one and it wasn't a simple single-session study. Since our study was made up of 7 sessions and each one had a very important function to fulfil.

In the first session, before the participants actually completed any training on the Japanese symbols they were required to complete a baseline assessment. We did this to make sure that they didn't have any prior knowledge of Japanese symbols. They could know a few but not too many otherwise we wouldn't have been able to tell if they had learnt them or known them from before.

After this baseline session and for the next five sessions, including the first one, the participant went through the training sessions. These were sessions where the participant had to learn 8 brand-new symbol-word pairs and the EEG was done in sessions 1 and 5 only. As well as these 5 training sessions happened the day after each other. The first session was always on a Monday and the fifth session was on the Friday.

Also, just for the sake of clarity, what a symbol-word pair is, is on the computer screen the participant was looking at there would be a Japanese symbol. Then before they were going to move onto the next one, they would see the English word translating that symbol.

It will make more sense later but I just wanted to clear that up right now.

Three days after the training sessions, the participants took part in the sixth session when they were exposed to all 40 Japanese symbol-word pairs again. We called this the Refresher session and it was designed to get rid of the primacy and recency effects, based on findings from Pyke et al. (2020).

The fact that the students were exposed to forty symbols instead of eight was the only difference between the training sessions the previous week and then the testing session took place 4 days after the sixth session. As well as whilst the participants knew the aim of the study, they were told not to rehearse stimuli outside of the sessions.

What Happened In Each Training Session?

When it came to the session itself, this worked by the Retrieval-Based Learning task being on the computer that the participant was facing and it actively involved me and the girl that I was working with.

Then the Japanese symbol-word pair would appear on the computer screen (thankfully we never ever had a problem with this technical area) and this pair was presented in a form of cued-recall where the participant was shown a symbol and asked to recall the English word belonging to the symbol.

And to be honest, if any participant got any on

the first lot then we were concerned and surprised because it meant that someone was really good.

However, like you and me, not a lot of people know Japanese so if they didn't know or remember what the symbol meant in English then they were asked to say 'Go'. This was marked as 'incorrect', and the next symbol was presented.

I'll mention why the word "Go" was used in a moment.

In addition, if a participant failed to say the English word within a few seconds then me and the girl I would working with say "Go" (sometimes rather forcefully by mistake) and then the computer went onto the next symbol.

Both of these wrong answers were marked as incorrect on the experimenter's screen and once the participant clicked 'J' on their keyboard, this then allowed the experimenter to mark their accuracy by a mouse-button click.

Personally, I will admit that because I did this Final Year Project in a group of other people, there were four of us total and only two of us worked on this EEG project. It was rather funny watching the three girls struggling to remember which mouse click was for correct and incorrect. That led to a lot of laughter in the early days of the project.

Thankfully that laughter continued very well for the entire year.

Moreover, when me or the girl had marked the response, on-screen feedback was shown to the participant. Meaning if the participant had given the wrong answer or said "go" then they needed to give us the correct answer out loud.

As well as after the participant had correctly said

a symbol-word pair three times in a row, we no longer needed to mark the accuracy on the computer, and there wasn't any more on-screen feedback given to the participant.

In reality, this was great fun and it was rather amazing watching the participant work away at the pairings because some people got in the 60s so they managed to do a word pairing one a second. But other people got into the 70s and 80s and our grand total was 95 symbols in a minute.

That was amazing to watch.

Anyway, the reason why they were able to get so high is because the lack of feedback and accuracy meant the participants were able to control the pace of the experiment. In turn this allowed them to cycle through the material at a faster speed.

But the participant would still make a mistake once in a while so if this did happen then we just said the correct answer.

How Did The Final Test Work?

I have to admit that I did love testing, I found it really fun, it was good to see the participants off and thank them for their time and I always wished them luck with their future studies. So if there was a choice between me doing testing and the girl doing EEG, I always went for testing because I loved it.

Honestly loved it.

As a result, the final testing session worked by "officially" three phases (but I'll explain what we really did in a minute because there two extra phases for someone else). The three sessions focused on different aspects of the participant's memory and therefore, performance. These phases were timed free recall, untimed cued recall, and timed cued recall.

In addition, each testing pack was automatically created by the software after the baseline and it was unique to each participant.

During the timed free recall phase, the participant was given a single minute to recall as many English names for the Japanese symbols as possible from the 40 they had learnt in the training sessions.

Now let me just say a lot of participants were understandable nightmares during this testing phase. Since for the past six sessions they had been using a computer and even if I said the following, they still firmly believed something would come up on the computer when the minute started:

I always said something along the lines of:

"On my phone, I'm going to record your voice for one minute because in the past six sessions, you're learnt 40 Japanese symbols. Now I want you to say the 40 English words belonging to those symbols please,"

I think I said a little more to make it clear but a lot of participants still didn't understand it first of all.

Furthermore, in the second session, the untimed cued-recall phase, all 40 symbols were shown on the computer screen in a random order and the participants were asked to recall the English word belonging to them without any time pressure.

This was really simple and easy but I didn't like it when participants focused for a thirty seconds on a symbol or two. We knew they didn't know it so it would have been nice if they simply went onto the next symbol.

Afterwards, for the final phase, the participant went through a timed cued-recall phase that was made up of two 1-min blocks where the symbols were presented randomly exactly like in the training sessions, except for the fact that feedback was never provided. As well as the incorrect and correct answers during all three cued-recall phases were marked by the researcher using a list generated prior.

That was the official end of our experiment but because this project was a joint one between cognitive psychology and Applied Behavioural Analysis, the ABA lecturer wanted us to do two more pieces of data collection for him which we were happy to do.

The next phase we asked participants to do was what was known as a Distractor phase and I'll introduce it how I explained it to participants because seeing how scared they got was great fun. It was the highlight of the testing session.

And yes I am that evil at times.

"It doesn't matter how well I explain this, you will not understand it until it comes up on the screen. But a Japanese Symbol will come up in the centre of the screen, that is the symbol we want the English word for. Yet surrounding it, will be tons of other symbols to confuse you. We want the English word for the one in the middle please,"

As you can imagine that scared participants and seeing their eyes widened in horror as the first symbol appeared was great fun.

Participants were actually a lot better at it than I imagined, so it was just some light-hearted fun as far as I was concerned but it was useful data for the ABA person at our university.

Then there was an endurance test, which was exactly the same as the 1-minute training blocks but it lasted three minutes. And boy, some participants could race through those minutes and always cause you to panic about marking things wrong.

Thankfully that didn't matter but it was very close at times. All part of the fun of research.

What Material Was Used In The Study?

As you can probably guess, there were both a lot and not a lot of materials needed in our study. Since I admit the procedure sounds long and complex and like it would require a lot of pieces of equipment, but thankfully it actually didn't.

Therefore, when it came to the equipment needed for the behavioural task itself, this required the use of a computer with two monitors. We needed this so a participant could see the materials on it and then us, the experimenters, needed another one so we could mark the responses right or wrong.

And let me tell you, that computer monitor situation was a complete and utter nightmare and that basically cursed the project for the first few weeks. It was so hard to get one of the monitors working. Sometimes the experimenter monitor wouldn't work, other times it was the participant monitor that failed, and hell, sometimes it was both.

It was a nightmare but one we really did laugh about.

Furthermore, the participant needed to use a keyboard to indicate their response and then me and the girl I was working with used a mouse to mark it correct or not.

After the free recall testing, we recorded the participants on our mobile phones and saved the audio file using an anonymous code and per ethical guidelines these recordings were deleted after the scores had been tallied up. As well as all of this was done and run on the software known as MATLAB

Version 2021b (MathWorks, 2021).

When it came to the EEG equipment itself, we used a setup involving a WaveGuard 10/10 layout EEG cap consisting of 32 Ag/AgCl electrode channels. As well as we used a standard measuring tape to measure the circumference of participants head for their cap size.

However, I will confess that the tape measure was next to useless, because we always measured their heads and looked up the cap sizes on the computer. Yet the cap sizes were always wrong so in the end we just looked at the participant and gave them the correct size cap by eye.

The measurements were useless.

After we got the measurements sorted out, we injected the conductive gel using a syringe with a blunt needle and it is this needle that was replaced for every single participant for the sake of hygiene.

Interesting thing about blunt needles and walking towards participants with a syringe in your hand, is make sure your participant is not scared of needles first of all.

Thankfully, we only had one participant that was scared of needles and she was horrible anyway. Yet what I did do was I explained to the participant that *we're going to inject the gel between the electrode and the scalp using a blunt needle.*

Then I always poked my hand with the blunt needle so they knew I wasn't lying.

And for the statistic lovers out there because the data wasn't normally distributed we used a Wilcoxon signed rank test was used to analyse this data.

Finally, the 48 Japanese symbols that we used in the course of the study were collected from https://www.learn-japanese-adventure.com/japanese-words.html. As a result of these symbols being developed as a stimuli bank in a previous study, so item difficulty and features were examined (Pyke, Lunau, & Javadi, submitted for publication). This meant we already knew this were an effective stimuli bank to use.

So now you know what we did in the study, how did this Retrieval-Based Learning impact recall ability?

HOW RETRIEVAL-BASED LEARNING IMPACT RECALL ABILITY?

Thankfully compare to the EEG results and data that I'll talk about in the next chapter, the behavioural findings which are the focus for this chapter were so easy to get.

However, because one of the main purposes of this book is to bring this study alive through my tales of hardship, interest and friendship that happened in the course of this study, I have to admit this data analysis was traumatic.

I mean it.

If you've read my book, *Third Year Survival Guide For Psychology Students*, you might have heard this already. Yet one of the reasons why I seriously recommend psychology students revise statistics before they start the data analysis section of their Final year project is simply because if you don't, you might struggle like we did.

Part of the problem was that I hadn't done stats

for two years because of my Placement Year, and the girl I was working with had never used SPSS before, and she had forgotten how to do the stats on R Studio.

I had no idea what R Studio was before my final year.

Therefore, let's just say it took us four hours to try and figure out how to do the stats to no avail and it was a long torturous process over the next few weeks as we struggled and eventually got the stats done.

Be prepared for statistical hell in your Final year.

Anyway let's see what the behavioural results were.

What Were The Behavioural Findings?

I have to admit that because my books are designed to be easy-to-understand, this will require some explaining.

So the first statistical test we ran was a 5 x 10 (Session x Block) Repeated Measurement ANOVA because we really wanted to examine the interaction between Session and Block on a participant's successful retrieval ability. Thankfully, the results were good because the main effects of Block were significant but this violated Mauchly's test ($p < .01$), so we had to correct this using the Greenhouse-Geisser correction. $F(1.49, 83.60)=588.57$, $MSE=46985.27$, $p <.001$. Whereas, the main effects of Session, $F(4, 224)=71.81$, $MSE=32127.71$, $p <.001$, and the main effects of Session x Block violated

Mauchly's test ($p < .01$), so again we had to do a little correction using our friend Greenhouse-Geisser correction. $F(9.43, 527.91) = 21.91$, MSE= 30.22, $p < .01$.

Overall, this ANOVA showed that Session and Block does have a significant effect on a participant's successful retrieval, with this being further supported by the significance of all pairwise comparisons ($p < .01$).

If these are just numbers to you at the moment, please relax because everything will make more sense in later chapters of the book.

Also, in the real Final Year Project there are a bunch of graphs and tables which I didn't include for book formatting purposes but I still want to mention that because they help to explain other things that are important to the project.

For example, in Figure 1a, there's a graph that showed the results of T-tests that we did and these found that participants had a significantly higher mean correct responses in Session 5 than Session 1 revealing $t(56) = 13.34$, $p < .001$, with the effect size was large with a Cohen's d of 0.59.

In addition, in Figure 1b that showed the Mean Correct Responses Between Session 1 Block 1 and Session 5 Block 1, this gave us further supporting evidence for our ANOVA because they showed the results of T-tests found participants had a significantly higher mean correct responses in Session 5 Block 1 than Session 1 Block 1 revealing $t(55) = 14.36$, p

<.001. As well as the effect size was large with a Cohen's d of 1.92.

Moreover, I decided to do another Figure too called Figure 1c that looked at the Mean Correct Responses Between Session 1 Block 10 and Session 5 Block 10 because I wanted to support the ANOVA findings even more. Therefore, I was happy to find that the results of T-tests found participants had a significantly higher mean correct responses in Session 5 Block 10 than Session 1 Block 10 revealing $t(55)=$ 10.15, $p < .001$ with the effect size was large with a Cohen's d of 1.35.

I'll talk about it more in later chapters, but all in all as the participant did more and more blocks and training sessions, they were getting better and better despite learning new stimuli.

When it came to the correlations, Figure 2 showed the correlation between a participant's mean number of correct answers in Session and Block and their Final Cued Recall scores, because this indicated successful retrieval. There was a strong positive correlation between the two variables, $r(49)= .584, p= (0.01)$ suggesting how well a participant does in Session and Block effects their Final Cued Recall scores.

Furthermore, Figure 3 showed the mean correct responses in each Block with error bars for the standard deviations of responses. This figure showed that participants got more correct responses as they were exposed to the Stimuli more as the Blocks progressed since the mean for Block 1 was 81.08 and Block 10 was 253.34.

Also, it has to be noted that this data and Figure were based on normal means and standard deviations as well as the bars correspond to 95% confidence intervals.

In addition, to further support the Figure 3 findings, Figure 4 looked at the Mean Correct Responses Cross Sessions 1-5 without looking at block. This Figure supported Figure 3 because it showed the standard deviations for mean correct responses per Session, demonstrating like Figure 3 as participants continued the task over the Sessions, they were getting more and more correct responses. The mean for Session 1 was 188 and the Session 5 was 369.18.

Also, same again, it has to be noted that this data and Figure were based on normal means and standard deviations as well as the bars correspond to 95% confidence intervals.

Another Nightmare

Just to break this up a little bit because I know this chapter and the next one (that is a lot, lot shorter) are more "setup" chapters because they are setting up the later chapters where we get into the meat of what these numbers actually mean and why they're important.

I actually wanted to mention something I think is very cool about SPSS and I know you can do this in R Studio, I just don't know how you do it yet.

We needed to create our own variable for our next ANOVA because it wasn't given to us in the raw data files. Therefore, me and the girl I was working with needed to use SPSS's table/ create variable function to create *Session Response Time* and *Block Response Time* for our ANOVA.

Yet the thing about any create variable function is that it is very precise, so if you put in your data wrong or you put a pre-existing variable in a column instead of a row then the programme refuses to do that.

I managed to work it out okay but the girl I was working with struggled a little. It was hard though.

Anyway, after we managed to create these two new variables we conducted a 5 x 10 (Session Response Time x Block Response Time) Repeated Measurement ANOVA so we were able to examine the interaction between Session Response Time and Block Response Time on Response Latency (also known as how long it takes for a participant to respond).

When we looked at the ANOVA outputs, Session Response Time, Block Response Time and the interaction between the two variables all violated Mauchly's test ($p < .01$), so at this point we had to look at our best friend the Greenhouse-Geisser correction so we could correct it.

Also, the main effects of Block Response Time were significant, $F(2.34,130.88)=33.64$, MSE=31.63, $p <.01$. The main effects of Session Response Time,

$F(3.12, 177.25)=71.44$, MSE=48.79, $p < .01$, and the main effects of Session Response Time x Block Response Time were $F(7.63, 427.45)= 2.08$, MSE= $0.44, p < .04$.

On the whole, this showed that Session Response Time and Block Response Time does have a significant effect on a participant's Response Latency, and this was further supported by the significance of all pairwise comparisons ($p < .01$).

Finally, and because at this point in the project I realised I couldn't resist a good graph, I created Figure 5 that showed the mean response times for participants between Session 1 and 5 that showed participants got faster as Session progresses. For example, the mean for Session 1 was 1.77 seconds and the mean for Session 5 was 1.19 seconds.

So we know how this study and experiment impacted behavioural data, but how did they impact brain activity?

HOW DOES RETRIEVAL-BASED LEARNING IMPACT BRAIN ACTIVITY?

To finish off the result section of the book, when it came to the EEG findings, we conducted an analysis (like everyone does) of the averaged EEG data and thankfully it showed a decrease in the frequency bands 4-8Hz. That's good for our study because it suggests that frontal midline theta (Rutishauser et al., 2010) decreased from the first to fifth training session.

Additionally, this was further supported by the Wilcoxon signed-rank test that demonstrated this difference was statistically significant ($Z=2.646$, $p = 0.008$). as well as the stats mentioned in this chapter were the average activity over the region of interest (frequency = [3, 8], and time = [400, 850] but not all electrodes demonstrated activity.

And the nightmare story about this data was that because EEG data analysis is so time-consuming. For example, you need to go through each and every data file, get rid of artefacts and made sure the data is clean. Each participant takes about two hours to go through so our supervisor was going to do most of the analysis for us.

That was brilliant and I will always be grateful for him.

However, to say my supervisor is a man with lots of free time is a silly thing to say so it took ages to get the data and results back from him. He gave us the data two days before the submission deadline, so to say we were a little concerned, stressed and panicked is a minor, minor understatement.

But what do these results mean in the grand scheme of things

HOW DOES RETRIEVAL-BASED LEARNING IMPACT TRANSFER LEARNING?

As we know from the first chapter of the book, my entire project was focusing on Transfer Learning and how this was increased by a participant using Retrieval-Based Learning. As well as we know from the results, it looks like Transfer learning did happen.

But what exactly do these results mean?

Because I really do understand that right now they might simply just look like numbers on a page without any meaning, context or life unless you've been living and breathing this for the past year.

Therefore, the proper way to say what I said above is that you know the study wanted to investigate Transfer Effects in Retrieval-Based Learning and we predicted that participants would increase across a time period because of Transfer Effects. Further, this study examined whether frontal-midline theta, measured as a function of effort, decreases between Session 1 and Session 5 predicting effort would decrease.

Then if we bring our results into this section, then they did support our hypothesis because our results did show that despite the participants learning new stimuli each session, there is a statistically significant improvement between Session 1 and Session 5 (see Figure 1).

In addition, this was further supported by our post-hoc tests being significant and Figure 3 and 4, because these Figures show further improvement to participants' scores across Sessions and Block.

This is important for our hypothesis because these results and Figures show how the participants did improve between Session 1 and Session 5 despite learning novel stimuli indicating Transfer Effects. As well as this was also supported by the statistically significant interaction between Session Response Time and Block Response on Response Latency and the supporting significant post-hoc tests. As a result of our results and Figures 2 and 5 showing that over the 5 Sessions, participants get quicker and more accurate at responding correctly.

And here's the kicker and why this is actually useful, this potentially shows the process of spreading activation occurring during a participant's search for answers on the Retrieval-Based Learning Task creating a multitude of retrieval cues to aid later recall, similar to the proposal and findings of Anderson (1996), Collins and Loftus (1975) and Raaijmakers and Shiffrin (1981) indicating Transfer Effects. Also, learning rate changes across Session indicating meta-learning (also known as Transfer Effect).

And that is why these results were really good, positive and they made writing up my discussion a lot easier compared to some of my other friends that were struggling to think of things to write because their results weren't significant.

When it comes to the literature and how our results match or don't match with it, I'm glad to say that our results do support previous literature about the Transfer and Testing Effect because as Pan and Rickard (2018) proposed participants are using their prior learning in the new context of each new session conducting the same task. This is what McDaniel (2007) found was needed for the Transfer Effect to occur. Also, this is similar to the findings of Pan and Rickard (2018) as they believed semantically-related information is what participants need to have actual recall later on, linking to the Testing Effect and Figure 2 as it shows the more correct responses a participant has in Session the more correct responses they give in Final Cued Recall tests.

In addition, our results in Figure 2 and 6 shows the process of spreading activation that occurs in initial testing (Session) and this increases the likelihood of this learnt stimuli being recalled later on, similar to several other studies (Carpenter, 2011; Chan, 2009; Chan et al., 2006; Cranney et al., 2009).

On the whole, the entire reason why this

discussion was good to write and I was rather positive during this was because theoretically our results provide additional supporting evidence for Transfer and Testing Effect and how these psychological principles impact memory retrieval during Retrieval-Based Learning tasks.

And because our results were significant, this made it easier to write up and talk about how it matched and fitted in with the current literature.

Yet what did the results mean for the changes in brain activity in the participants?

THE MEANING OF BRAIN ACTIVITY CHANGES

We know from the result section that there were in fact changes in the participant's brain activity between the different sessions, but what does this actually mean?

These results helped us to support our second hypothesis due to our results did thankfully find a significant decrease in frontal midline theta between training session 1 and training session 5. As a result, this does suggest that Frontal midline theta does modulate or control a participant's effort in Retrieval-Based Learning.

In terms of past literature and other research findings, this is widely supported because it does match previous literature on the topic. Due to we did find a decrease in Frontal midline theta that led to successful long-term memory encoding. Similar to the findings of Khader et al. (2010) and our findings suggest that EEG data can be used to investigate effort as Nguyen et al. (2018) proposed.

Although, one thing I do like about science and this is something that the anti-science crowd fail to realise, is that there is no such thing as empirical Truth. We can only test out theories and get as close to the truth as possible.

As a result, our findings weren't supported by all other studies. One example of this is from Gevins et al. (1997) who found an increase in both Alpha power and Frontal midline theta after task practice where this study only found an decrease in Frontal midline theta. Therefore, our results are conflicting to this study.

Although, this could be because Gevins didn't use a Retrieval-based Learning paradigm in their study or task type, but this still demonstrates our results add to the body of literature supporting Frontal midline theta modulates effort in learning and additional literature suggests Frontal midline theta is highly related to cognitively demanding tasks and/or tasks requiring high mental concentration (Doppelmayr et al., 2008; Ishii et al., 2014).

Another reason why our findings are important to the literature is because our finding of a decrease in Frontal midline theta does suggest that whilst participants maximise their correct response scores, the participants apply meta-learning (Transfer Effects) protocols to minimise the cortical resources required for the task.

As well as this neurological data supports

previous behavioural studies demonstrating the effectiveness of RBL tasks in helping participant learning because our task enabled participants to complete the task more effectively by practising and this resulted in reducing the time and effort needed for successful retrievals.

On the whole, whilst the theoretical implications are mixed because our results fit with some, but not all, literature. This paper further supports the argument of it is Frontal midline theta, not alpha power modulating effort in RBL.

So as nice as all this theoretical stuff is, how could this actually help people in the real-world?

HOW CAN RETRIEVAL-BASED LEARNING BE APPLIED IN THE REAL WORLD?

One of my massive problems that I am very adamant on is psychology research has to be able to help people, improve lives and help make the world a better place. Yes, I know exactly how idealistic that little belief is but to me that is the entire point of psychology and all of science.

Therefore, one of my minor problems with cognitive psychology is that there is a lot of amazing theoretical work being done behind the scenes to truly help up understand how the different cognitive processes work.

Yet sometimes I feel like cognitive psychology does fall down when it comes to applied areas.

So when I found out that Retrieval-Based Learning could actually be useful in the real world I was extremely happy and I am rather excited about telling you these practical implications.

For example, I'm very happy to say that our research findings do actually have a lot of practical implications. Not only because our research adds to the validity and wider literature support for Retrieval-Based Learning interventions, this can be used to support Retrieval-Based Learning in education contexts, for example.

And it's this use in education that really interests me because Retrieval-Based Learning has a history of use in educational settings covering a range of settings. For instance, Sanders et al. (2019) showed how Retrieval-Based Learning tasks can effectively teach medical students human anatomy better than students passively exposed to learnt material with the authors noting how Retrieval-Based Learning tasks can be applied to any educational setting.

Furthermore, this has additional research support from other medical school studies, like Sya'ban et al. (2021) and different sectors within education from general education (Buchin and Mulligan, 2023) and special education settings (Gordon, 2020).

On the whole, these findings do help to show that our results can very well be applied to real-world problems by helping students learn better. As well as I think you could easily argue that our findings could have implications throughout the education sector from the lower years in primary and secondary school all the way up to university-level students. Also, Retrieval-Based Learning does have the empirical backing in the literature to help all these students improve the amount of learnt material later recalled.

Which as psychology students and professionals, I think we can all admit that would be rather nice.

Also, because I was doing a more specialised clinical psychology degree instead of a standard psychology degree, in order for me to pass the Final Year Project, I had to link this topic to clinical psychology or the university did have to fail me.

Thankfully, the university did admit the link could be very, very tenuous and whilst I don't think this link is weak, I am very happy that I was still given the freedom to explore whatever I wanted.

Consequently, I am happy to say that Retrieval-Based Learning tasks do have a good number of uses within clinical psychology because RBL is commonly used in word-learning contexts for children with learning disabilities.

One example of this Retrieval-Based Learning can be seen in a review by Gordon (2020) who found modern empirical evidence shows Retrieval-Based Learning can enhance word learning for children with learning disorders with there being guidance for clinicians on how to effectively apply Retrieval-Based Learning for word learning. As a result, Gordan (2020)'s findings are important for our results because this study used a word-learning task to teach students Japanese symbols, suggesting our results have direct implications for children with language disorders. This is further supported by other studies, like Haebig et al. (2019), Leonard et al. (2019), Leonard et al.

(2020) and Leonard and Deevy (2020).

Also, those additional studies and I suppose in an indirect way our study supports this point to, that Retrieval-Based Learning tasks help both typically-developing children and those with a language disorder learn novel word stimuli and experience long-term retention.

Overall, a wide range of studies help to show how our results can be used to implement real-world interventions to help children affected by developmental language disorders enhance their word learning, and given how language skills are highly predictable of a child's ability to read and success at school (Dickinson & Tabors, 2001; McCardle et al., 2001; Snow, Burns & Griffin, 2005; Snow et al., 1999; Stanovich et al., 1986; Storch & Whitehurst, 2001; Walker, Greenwood, Hart & Carta, 1994), this is an important problem needing an intervention. Retrieval-Based Learning tasks could be the intervention as showed in our results and those of other studies.

Although, I have to admit everything so far in this book has been very rosy and focused on the positive, what could the limitations of our study be?

LIMITATION OF THE STUDY

Because psychology is a science and I personally believe that the most dangerous thing to a science is not learning, not improving and not building on past research, I have to admit that I rather like critical thinking sections.

Since they give us, mere students, a chance to have our say in the research of psychology. They give us a chance to speak up about something we don't like about a research methodology, a practice or something that, using evidence to back us up of course.

Also, we all know that a student's ability to get a high grade is important and is half-determined by their ability to think critically about the research literature and how to improve the current state of psychology.

That's why I'm going to take you through the following critical thinking points including what I actually put in my project, why I personally did it and maybe something else interesting along the way.

The Importance Of Control Groups

Personally, if you've been a long time reader or listener of The Psychology World Podcast then you might know I am very anal about control groups. I love them, they are needed and they are absolutely critical to good research.

This was especially hammered home to me during my academic placement year where I had to research the Gamification of Autism and by God does that literature not even know the meaning of Control Groups.

Therefore, when it came to our study having several limitations that very much needed to be addressed in future research. Control groups were always going to be the top of my list because control groups are needed so researchers know if an intervention is working and these effects can be separated from the effects of other interventions (Pithon, 2013). This is very similar to another favourite methodology of mine because Randomised Controlled Trials (RCT) in clinical psychology research allow researchers to benefit from RCT being the most robust and empirical method for establishing whether a cause-and-effect relationships exists (Bhide et al., 2018).

That is just beyond critical in good psychology research.

However, because our study didn't use a control group we only know that our findings did show our

Retrieval-Based learning task was helpful in participant learning and successful retrieval, yet we cannot separate these effects from other interventions because this study cannot say if the successful retrieval was a result of our task or them doing a learning intervention regardless of the type used.

That's why I'm adamant that any future research absolutely needs to use control groups to make sure the study's results are from the Retrieval-Based Learning intervention and not other variables.

Neuroelectronic Limitation

When I was researching this topic I wanted to highlight that the EEG could be a fault in itself and I managed to do that by looking at the following limitation.

As a result, whilst our study found a decrease in Frontal Midline Theta was related to learning and more successful retrievals later on, we flat out didn't investigate the participant's neuroelectric activity during the testing phase and since this study didn't use a control group this study could not investigate cognitive effort in differentially difficult tasks. This would have given us more data to support our conclusions with and it would have made our study fit with additional literature.

Translation.

Also, for the non-cognitive psychology people who haven't been living and breathing this topic for a year of their life. What this means is the we don't know what happened to the brain activity during the training sessions outside of session 1 and session 5. For example, was there a particular day the brain activity changed? Was there a rapid or gradual decline in Frontal Midline Theta? Or did the decline take all week to develop?

Who knows?

Also, it's important to note that because of the lack of a control group, we cannot say that because the Retrieval-Based Learning task was "harder" compared to another task that this "hardness" was what led to greater difficulty caused a greater decline. Because we have nothing to compare it too.

This criticism does have research support behind it because Berry and Thompson (1978) found rabbits who showed higher theta activity learnt faster than rabbits with higher brain frequencies. (Again they had a control group to compare their results too) Also, Mussel et al. (2016) found theta power reflects cognitive effort on tasks differing in difficulty and this is predictive of performance on these tasks. So together these studies demonstrate neuroelectric activity can be used to investigate motivational and effort mechanisms underpinning active learning tasks. As a result, whilst our study didn't look at these concepts, future research should investigate differences in neuroelectric differences between experimental and control groups to see whether such oscillatory differences can predict differences in performance to further add to the RBL literature.

<u>Is One Week Enough?</u>

Another one of my little soapboxes when it comes to research is very much about longitudinal studies. I think they are fascinating, brilliant and if they weren't so expensive or difficult to get participants for (even our study was a little difficult to get sign-ups for) then I would be happy to support something that made a longitudinal study a compulsory part of research. If it was appropriate for the research topic of course.

Anyway, as I told you earlier, our study made use of a 1-week post-test element so this allowed us to understand the long-term impacts of our Retrieval-Based Learning intervention on participant performance. Although, I did have one problem with this 1 week period.

I believe that future research should make use of longer post-intervention periods to further understand the long-term effects of RBL.

Since the problem is, currently, this study can only say with empirical evidence, Retrieval-Based Learning is effective for one week following the intervention. Anything longer is guessing. Also, this is a larger criticism of the RBL literature because a plethora of studies only use one-week post-intervention posts, like Agarwal et al. (2008), Karpicke and Grimaldi (2012) and Roediger and Butler (2011). Therefore, this limitation needs to be addressed in the literature because currently the longer term effects of Retrieval-Based Learning are unknown.

Also, it is arguable the work of Sheffield and

Hudson (2006), Memon et al. (1997) and Hudson (1990) nullifies this limitation because research shows improved retrieval of novel events and improved memory 8- and 12-weeks after learning. Yet these studies didn't use Retrieval-Based Learning tasks making the results difficult to compare and the research sample was 18-months old infants, pre-schoolers and elementary pupils, not adults. Hence, this limitation remains.

Overall, future research should use different experimental groups with different post-intervention time periods, allowing researchers to learn if there is a limit or optimal gap between training and testing.

I know this is a very nit-picky limitation because as I said earlier, this is one of my soapboxes and I do enjoy learning about behaviour over time.

So moving onto the final chapter, what are the conclusions we can draw from this study?

CONCLUSION

As we start to wrap up the book, I have to admit it has been a lot of fun looking at my dissertation through a new lens and writing up the joys and problems that I had along the way. I did this because I wanted to show people that your dissertation doesn't have to be scary and I also wanted to show that lab work in psychology can and is a lot of fun if you allow it to be with a positive mindset.

Also, I won't deny that Retrieval-Based Learning is actually a very interesting topic and whilst I will probably never ever look at it again, I've had a great year looking into it and helping to do some research into the topic.

In terms of what the actual project concluded, as you can imagine, we did provide evidence showing that a Retrieval-Based Learning task is useful in learning and this study explores several behavioural and neurological mechanisms for why this occurs.

I also concluded that these reasons for our

results were mainly as a result of meta-learning or Transfer Effect because this effect promotes successful retrieval by applying learning across similar contexts requiring less effort to learn. All of this was very similar with our results and Transfer Effect is widely supported in the literature as an underlying principle of learning (Pan & Rickard, 2018).

As well as our results do have valuable implications for RBL theories, like Transfer Appropriate Processing theory and Long-term Potentiation, because this is the first time neuroevidence on Transfer Effects has been conducted, directing future research towards using control groups, longitudinal methodology and investigating neural oscillations during the testing phase.

However, maybe one of my favourite things about this project is that this does have important applications in the real-world and surprisingly enough (don't tell my supervisor I said that) Retrieval-Based Learning can be used to help improve lives. Since I mentioned how our results can be practically applied in clinical and educational settings were using active learning procedures to boost learning and performance is on the rise (Wirth & Perkins, 2008).

And I have to admit that is honestly what I love about psychology and research, I have always said that I would never ever be an academic and I would never want to be a researcher for living. Especially because of how badly universities treat their employees, like how I talk about in Careers In Psychology, yet research is fun, interacting with participants is fun and of course 99% of the research anyone does will never be that life-changing.

But it could be.

Research is the lifeblood of the modern world. Research allows people to get psychological help, it allows businesses to thrive and it allows us to improve lives all because you or an academic thought about researching something in a lab one day.

What I am saying is that research isn't a bad thing and doing research for your dissertation is actually a brilliant chance for you to have a little fun if you go into it with a positive mindset.

But my larger point is that if you love research, if you love academic writing, if you love working with participants. Then go for it. Do not let that passion die, nurture it and make sure you continue to enjoy academia.

No one will lie to you and say it's easy but we need more passionate researchers in psychology, because all the problems in the world can be solved by passionate people, whether you're a researcher or not.

I hope you learnt something and I hope to see you in another book soon.

Have a great day everyone.

Investigating Oscillatory Activity Associated Transfer Learning

School of Psychology, University of Kent

PSYC 6003: Clinical Psychology Project

Word Count: 4,723

Abstract

Transfer Effect has been proposed to explain how retrieval practise can improve learning, although there is no neuroevidence for this behavioural mechanism. This study proposes using theta brain oscillation (4-8 Hz) can quantify effort allowing the longer-term impacts of Retrieval-based learning to be explained using neuroevidence for the first time. Furthermore, this study suggests Long-Term Potentiation and Neural Efficiency Hypothesis can explain why Transfer Effect occurs from a neuroevidence standpoint. This study used a mixed factorial design (N=50) where participants took part in a learning task extended over several sessions where they continuously retrieved target materials. Then participants where assessed on their long-term retention of this material. The study demonstrated despite participants learning novel stimuli in each session, the task led to an increase in performance across the sessions, supporting the presence of Transfer Effect. Lastly, the study showed Frontal Midline Theta was associated with effort as it decreased from the first to last learning session, showing the participants found the task easier over time. Suggesting Frontal Midline Theta is a useful quantifier of effort and does provide neuroevidence for Transfer Effect. Then implications on the Retrieval-Based learning and Transfer Effect literature are discussed, highlighting how biological processes underpin this behavioural process, and how this links to meta-learning protocols used by the participant.

Investigating Oscillatory Activity Associated Transfer Learning

Learning is critical in everyday life from learning how to ride a bike to how to revise effectively for exams to how to drive a car, learning is everywhere, and learning requires several cognitive skills including memory retrieval as retrieval enhances learning (Roediger & Karpicke, 2006), leading to the development of retrieval-based learning (RBL) tasks, were learners' re-access newly learnt stimuli by undergoing tests. Typically, participants in an RBL task have an initial learning phase, where learners are tested on said stimuli, next is a testing phase, where the learners are tested on this material. RBL tasks utilise various combinations of these study-test blocks. Such as, STST, STTT, etc (Pyke et al., 2021). In control conditions, learners will not be tested on learnt material and all learners complete a final assessment to measure their overall learning, with these assessments taking place minutes (Smith et al., 2013) or months (Carpenter et al., 2009) after the previous phases. RBL tasks are beneficial for various populations, including patients (Friedman et al., 2017), children (Lipowski et al., 2014) and older adults (Coane, 2013) and RBL reliably shows increased long-term retention of learnt stimuli compared to study-only conditions (Agarwal et al., 2008; Fazio & Marsh, 2019; Karpicke & Grimaldi, 2012; Roediger & Butler, 2011).

The concept of learning via retrieval started in the early 20th century (Abbott, 1909; Gates, 1917, Spitzer, 1939) and Bjork's (1994) Desirable Difficulties Framework fits with RBL as it proposes an effective way to improve long-term retention of learnt stimuli is to introduce a desirable amount of difficulty (effort) whilst learning. Several models have been put forward to explain the efficacy of RBL. For example, Transfer Appropriate Processing (TAP) or Transfer Effect is the proactive use of prior learning in a novel context (Pan & Rickard, 2018) with a novel context potentially referring to any situation that is somehow different to the content the learning originally took place in (McDaniel, 2007). For example, a different test type, topic or goal (Barnett & Ceci, 2002). This links to effort because the TAP proposes a process of spreading activation occurs during the search for answers on a test (Anderson, 1996; Collins & Loftus, 1975; Raaijmakers & Shiffrin, 1981), creating multiple retrieval cues to aid later recall. This results in the testing effect (Pan & Rickard, 2018) and Pan and Rickard (2018) believed Transfer Effects could result from the same mechanism, because semantically-related information similar to previously learnt stimuli needs to be recalled on a transfer test. Therefore, the process of spreading activation that presumably occurs during the initial testing increases the likelihood this learnt information will be recallable as well (Carpenter, 2011; Chan, 2009; Chan, McDermott, & Roediger, 2006; Cranney, Ahn, McKinnon, Morris, & Watts, 2009) suggesting participants implicitly employ techniques to carry out learning resulting in effort likely being reduced. Overall, Pan and Rickard (2018) concluded test-enhanced learning could yield transfer performance substantially better than non-testing re-exposure conditions. This supports this paper's examination as our RBL task will help to provide further evidence for the efficacy of test-enhanced learning and Transfer Effects.

Furthermore, there are several biological processes that could be responsible for Transfer Effects. For example, Long-term Potentiation (LTP) is the strengthening of synapses based on recent neural activation producing a long-lasting increase in information transmission between two neurons (Cooke and Bliss, 2006). LTP underpins neuroplasticity (Bliss and Collingridge, 1993), this relates to Transfer Effect because memories are believed to be encoded according to synaptic strength. Hence, LTP is a major mechanism behind learning and memory (Bliss and Collingridge, 1993; Cooke and Bliss, 2006) possibly aiding in the process of spreading activation and creating retrieval cues for later recall as TAP proposes. Also, the Neural Efficiency Hypothesis proposes during a cognitive task, people with higher brain activation compared to low activation will be more successful at the task (Dunst et al., 2014) suggesting performance differences are caused by differences in the efficacy of a person's neural processing (Neubauer and Fink, 2009). Hence, this supports Transfer Effect because it would explain neurologically why some participants are better at a task compared to others, and presumably not as able to apply learning across similar contexts when learning new stimuli. Therefore, this paper will investigate transfer effect using Electroencephalogram (EEG) to provide supporting evidence for the neural basis of transfer effects, something not done until now.

In addition, EEG measures neuron electrical

activity in the brain (Wu et al., 2016) and depending on the type of memory being retrieved different brain areas require different neural oscillations for successful encoding (Khader et al., 2010). For instance, stronger alpha activity was found in occipital-to-parietal scalp sites for subsequently remembered stimuli, and stronger theta power was found for subsequently remembered stimuli over parietal-to-central electrodes. Hence this suggests alpha and theta oscillations modulate successful LTM encoding (Khader et al., 2010) and theta activity is involved in working memory maintenance (Hsieh et al., 2014) with frontal theta oscillations playing a causal role in prioritizing WM representations (Riddle et al., 2020). Also, Nguyen et al. (2018) demonstrates how EEG can be used to quantify 'effort' in empirical investigations allowing this paper to empirically measure the effects of RBL on a participant's neuroactivity.

Furthermore, neural brain activity has a multitude of effects on WM which is involved in learning (Reber and Kotovsky, 1997; Schuler et al., 2011). For instance, frontal midline theta is critical for cognitive controls in and acts functionally different depending on task demands (Eschmann et al., 2018), and alpha brainwaves increase significantly during retrieval compared to demand and attentional tasks, and increasing alpha synchronisation with memory retrieval increases good memory performance (Klimesch et al., 1993). Suggesting a decrease in alpha synchronisation always leads to a decrease in memory performance, and supporting the role of brain oscillatory activity in memory. Further, when theta power increases during the memory encoding of words, more words are remembered later on and alpha power decreases during encoding yet did not always show significant differences in the alpha band between words remembered and not remembered (Klimesch and Doppelmayr, 1996). These human results are supported by animal studies as well, since Jutras and Buffalo (2014) demonstrated changes in medial temporal lobe activity across multiple frequency bands associated with stimulus novelty, familiarity, memory reactivation, temporal resolution, associative learning, and memory encoding provided evidence that neural oscillations could influence interactions between neurons during learning to encourage the formation of functional networks ready for later activation for consolidation or retrieval. Hence lending supporting evidence to how transfer effects could work in the brain.

Therefore, whilst no paper until now has provided neuro-evidence for Transfer Effect, this paper aims to see how the brain reflects the amount of effort university students put into learning because of transfer effect techniques by measuring differences in EEG activity in Session 1 and Session 5. This paper hypotheses theta activity will decrease in participants from Session 1 to Session 5. Also this paper seeks to examine performance improvement over time, predicting despite participants learning novel stimuli in each training session, they will improve between Session 1 to Session 5, indicating transfer effects.

Methods

Participants

G*Power 3.1.9.7 was used to run a priori power analysis and as a result 50 participants were recruited using volunteer sampling through the Research Participation Scheme at the University of Kent with an age range of 19-32 years old (M= 20) and 43 were female. Exclusion criterion for the study included any previous knowledge of any logographic language, being left-handed, having learning difficulties, like dyslexia and not being 17-32 years old. Yet participant nationality and ethnicity demographics were not collected. All participants received payment for their participation. The payment was £10 for RPS participants.

Design

Our quasi-experimental study used a mixed factorial design, with one ratio and two categorical independent variables (IVs), these were: Performance, Session, and Block. The dependent variables (DVs) for the study were Successful Retrievals, Response Latency, Untimed Cued-Recall Score, and Theta Power. For operationalisations of the variables, see Statistical Analyses, with a controlled variable being the day on which each session occurred.

Materials

Task Equipment

Our RBL-variation task required the use of a computer with two monitors, one for the participant to see the material on, and another for the experimenter to mark the responses correct/incorrect. The participants were never able to see the experimenter's screen. The participant used a keyboard to indicate their response, whilst the experimenter marked this using a mouse. During free recall testing, participants were recorded using the experimenter's mobile phone; this was labelled using an anonymous code and the recordings were deleted after the scores had been tallied. The software used to run the task was MATLAB Version 2021b (MathWorks, 2021).

EEG Equipment

EEG was set up with a WaveGuard 10/10 layout EEG cap consisting of 32 Ag/AgCl electrode channels. A standard measuring tape was used to measure the circumference of participants head for their cap size. The conductive gel was inserted into the electrodes using a syringe, the tip of which was replaced for each new participant. Also, a Wilcoxon signed rank test was used to analyse this data because the data was not normally distributed.

Stimuli

The stimuli used included 48 Japanese symbols, all of which were collected from https://www.learn-japanese-adventure.com/japanese-words.html. A previous study, that developed the current stimuli bank, examined the features and difficulties of these items (Pyke, Lunau, & Javadi, submitted for publication).

Procedure

General Procedure

The study consisted of 7 sessions. In the initial session, before completing any training, participants were asked to complete a baseline assessment to ensure that they had no prior knowledge of the symbols used in the study. During the first 5 training sessions, 8 novel symbol-word pairs were learnt by the participants, and EEG was administered in sessions 1 and 5 only. The first 5 training sessions were consecutive to each other. The sixth training session took place 3 days after session 5, where participants were exposed to all the symbols they had learnt in the previous sessions. This was done to control for primacy and recency effects, based on findings from Pyke et al. (2020). Aside from this, session 6 followed the same general procedure as the previous five. The testing session took place 4 days after session 6. Whilst participants knew the aim of the study, they were told not to rehearse stimuli outside of the sessions.

Task Procedure

The RBL task was completed on a computer and actively involved another person (the experimenter). The Japanese symbol-English word pairs were presented in the form of cued-recall, the participant was shown a symbol and asked to recall the corresponding English word. If participants did not remember or know the English word, they were asked to say 'Go'. This was marked as 'incorrect', and the next symbol was presented. If the participant failed to respond within a few seconds, they were prompted by the experimenter to say 'Go' and continue onto the next symbol. This was recorded as an incorrect response as well. Along with every response, the participant was asked to click 'J' on their keyboard, which allowed the experimenter to mark their accuracy by a mouse-button click. Once the experimenter had marked the response, on-screen feedback was given to the participant. If they responded with the incorrect word, or said 'go', they were required to repeat the correct answer out loud. After the participant had correctly answered a symbol-word pair three consecutive times, the experimenter no longer needed to indicate accuracy, because it was assumed to be correct, and no further feedback was provided. This gave control of pace to the participant, allowing them to cycle through the material at a faster speed. If an incorrect answer was given at any point during this stage, the experimenter would interrupt the participant with the correct answer.

Final Test

The testing session consisted of three phases testing different aspects of participants' memory performance: timed free recall, untimed cued recall, and timed cued recall. The "testing pack" was specific to each participant. In the timed free recall phase, participants were given 1min to recall the English names for the symbols they had learnt during the six training sessions. In the untimed cued-recall phase, all 40 symbols were presented in random order and participants were asked to recall the corresponding English word without any time pressure. The timed cued-recall phase consisted of two 1-min blocks in which symbols were presented randomly. In all cued-recall phases, symbols were shown in the same manner as in the training sessions, except feedback was never provided. Incorrect and correct answers during all three cued-recall phases were marked by the researcher using a list generated prior.

Results

Behavioural Findings

We conducted a 5 x 10 (Session x Block) Repeated Measurement ANOVA examining the interaction between Session and Block on successful retrieval. The main effects of Block were significant but this violated Mauchly's test ($p < .01$), this was corrected with Greenhouse-Geisser correction. $F(1.49, 83.60)=588.57$, MSE=46985.27, $p < .001$. The main effects of Session, $F(4, 224)=71.81$, MSE=32127.71, $p < .001$, and the main effects of Session x Block violated Mauchly's test ($p < .01$), this was corrected with Greenhouse-Geisser correction. $F(9.43, 527.91)= 21.91$, MSE= 30.22, $p < .01$, demonstrating Session and Block does have a significant effect on a participant's successful retrieval. Further confirmed by the significance of all pairwise comparisons ($p < .01$).

Figure 1a shows the results of T-tests finding participants had a significantly higher mean correct responses in Session 5 than Session 1 revealing $t(56)= 13.34$, $p <.001$. The effect size was large with a Cohen's d of 0.59.

Figure 1b- Mean Correct Response Between Session 1 Block 1 and Session 5 Block 1

Figure 1b further supports the ANOVA findings by showing the results of T-tests finding participants had a significantly higher mean correct responses in Session 5 Block 1 than Session 1 Block 1 revealing $t(55)= 14.36$, $p <.001$. The effect size was large with a Cohen's d of 1.92.

Figure 1c- *Mean Correct Response Between Session 1 Block 10 and Session 5 Block 10*

Figure 1c shows the results of T-tests finding participants had a significantly higher mean correct responses in Session 5 Block 10 than Session 1 Block 10 revealing $t(55)= 10.15$, $p <.001$. The effect size was large with a Cohen's d of 1.35.

Figure 2- Correlation Between Mean Correct Responses And Final Cued Recall Scores

Figure 2 shows the correlation between a participant's mean number of correct answers in Session and Block and their Final Cued Recall scores, indicating successful retrieval. There was a strong positive correlation between the two variables, $r(49)= .584$, $p= (0.01)$ suggesting how well a participant does in Session and Block effects their Final Cued Recall scores.

Figure 3- Mean Correct Responses Between Block 1-10

Figure 3 shows the mean correct responses in each Block with error bars for the standard deviations of responses, showing participants got more correct responses as they were exposed to the Stimuli more as the Blocks progressed since the mean for Block 1 was 81.08 and Block 10 was 253.34.

Note. Based on normal means and standard deviations. Bars correspond to 95% confidence intervals.

Figure 4- Mean Correct Responses Cross Sessions 1-5

Figure 4 supports Figure 3 by showing the standard deviations for mean correct responses per Session, demonstrating like Figure 3 as participants continue the task over the Sessions, they get more correct responses. The mean for Session 1 was 188 and the Session 5 was 369.18.

Note. Based on estimated marginal means. Bars correspond to 95% confidence intervals.

We conducted a 5 x 10 (Session Response Time x Block Response Time) Repeated Measurement ANOVA examining the interaction between Session Response Time and Block Response Time on Response Latency. Session Response Time, Block Response Time and the interaction between the two variables violated Mauchly's test ($p < .01$), this was corrected with Greenhouse-Geisser correction. The main effects of Block Response Time were significant, $F(2.34,130.88)=33.64$, $MSE=31.63$, $p <.01$. The main effects of Session Response Time,

$F(3.12, 177.25)=71.44$, MSE=48.79, $p <.01$, and the main effects of Session Response Time x Block Response Time were $F(7.63, 427.45)= 2.08$, MSE= 0.44, $p < .04$, demonstrating Session Response Time and Block Response Time does have a significant effect on a participant's Response Latency. Both of these variables violated Mauchly's test ($p < .01$) so Greenhouse-Geisser corrections were needed. Further confirmed by the significance of all pairwise comparisons ($p < .01$).

Figure 5- Mean Response Times Between Session 1-5

Figure 5 shows the mean response times for participants between Session 1 and 5 showing participants get faster as Session progresses. The mean for Session 1 was 1.77 seconds and the mean for Session 5 was 1.19 seconds.

Electrophysiological Findings

Analysis of the averaged EEG data showed a decrease in the frequency bands 4-8Hz suggesting frontal midline theta (Rutishauser et al., 2010), from the first to fifth training session as showed in Figure 6. The Wilcoxon signed-rank test demonstrated this difference was statistically significant ($Z=2.646$, $p = 0.008$). These statistics are the average activity over the region of interest (frequency = [3, 8], and time = [400, 850]. Although not all electrodes demonstrated activity.

Figure 6- *Neuroelectric Comparisons Between Sessions One and Five*

A- *the average of all participants for electrode Fp1*

B - the average of all participants for electrode Fz.

Note. Figure 7 shows the activity and differences in both sessions with the dashed rectangle showing the region of analysis.

Discussion

The current study set out to investigate Transfer Effects in RBL predicting participants would increase across a time period because of Transfer Effects. Further, this study examined whether frontal-midline theta, measured as a function of effort, decreases between Session 1 and Session 5 predicting effort would decrease.

This supported our hypothesis by demonstrating despite participants learning new stimuli each session, there is a statistically significant improvement between Session 1 and Session 5 (see Figure 1). This was further supported by our post-hoc tests being significant and Figure 3 and 4, because these Figures show further improvement to participants' scores across Sessions and Block. Hence, as this paper set out to investigate, our results show participants do improve between Session 1 and Session 5 despite learning novel stimuli indicating Transfer Effects. Further, this hypothesis is supported by the statistically significant interaction between Session Response Time and Block Response on Response Latency and the supporting significant post-hoc tests. Due to our results and Figures 2 and 5 demonstrate over the 5 Sessions, participants get quicker and more accurate at responding correctly potentially showing the process of spreading activation occurring during a participant's search for answers on the RBL Task creating a multitude of retrieval cues to aid later recall, similar to the proposal and findings of Anderson (1996), Collins and Loftus (1975) and Raaijmakers and Shiffrin (1981) indicating Transfer Effects. Also, learning rate changes across Session indicating meta-learning (Transfer Effect).

Moreover, our results support previous literature about the Transfer and Testing Effect because as Pan and Rickard (2018) proposed participants are using their prior learning in the new context of each new session conducting the same task. This is what McDaniel (2007) found was needed for the Transfer Effect to occur. Also, this is similar to the findings of Pan and Rickard (2018) as they believed semantically-related information is what participants need to have actual recall later on, linking to the Testing Effect and Figure 2 as it shows the more correct responses a participant has in Session the more correct responses they give in Final Cued Recall tests. Moreover, our results in Figure 2 and 6 demonstrates the process of spreading activation that occurs in initial testing (Session) increases the likelihood of this learnt stimuli being called later on, similar to several other studies (Carpenter, 2011; Chan, 2009; Chan et al., 2006; Cranney et al., 2009). Overall, theoretically our results provide additional supporting evidence for Transfer and Testing Effect and how these psychological principles impact memory retrieval during RBL tasks.

Further, this study did support our second hypothesis because this study find did a significant decrease in frontal midline theta (Fmθ) between T1 and T5 suggesting Fmθ modulates effort in RBL. This matches previous literature because this study found a decrease in Fmθ which lead to successful LTM encoding. These findings are similar to Khader et al. (2010) and our findings suggest EEG data can be used to investigate effort as Nguyen et al. (2018) proposed. However, our findings do not support other studies. For instance, Gevins et al. (1997) found an increase in both Alpha power and Fmθ after task practice where this study only found an increase in Fmθ. Therefore, our results are conflicting to this study. This could be because Gevins did not use a RBL paradigm in the study or task type, but this still demonstrates our results add to the body of literature supporting Fmθ modulates effort in learning and additional literature suggests Fmθ is highly related to cognitively demanding tasks and/or tasks requiring high mental concentration (Doppelmayr et al., 2008; Ishii et al., 2014).

Moreover, our finding of a decrease in Fmθ suggests whilst participants maximise their correct response scores, the participants apply meta-learning (Transfer Effects) protocols to minimise the cortical resources required for the task. This neurological data supports previous behavioural studies demonstrating the effectiveness of RBL tasks in aiding participant learning because our task enabled participants to complete the task more effectively by practising and this resulted in reducing the time and effort needed for successful retrievals. Therefore, whilst the theoretical implications are mixed because our results fit with some, but not all, literature. This paper further supports the argument of it is Fmθ, not alpha power modulating effort in RBL.

Our research findings have a plethora of practical implications. Since our research findings add to the validity and wider literature support for RBL interventions, this can be used to support RBL in education contexts, for example. RBL has a history of use in educational settings covering a range of settings. Sanders et al. (2019) demonstrated how RBL tasks can effectively teach medical students human anatomy better than students passively exposed to learnt material with the authors noting how RBL tasks can be applied to any educational setting. This has additional research support from other medical school studies, like Sya'ban et al. (2021) and different sectors within education from general education (Buchin and Mulligan, 2023) and special education settings (Gordon, 2020). Therefore, these findings show this paper's results could have implications throughout the education sector from the lower years in primary and secondary school all the way up to university-level students. RBL has the empirical backing in the literature to help all these students improve the amount of learnt material later recalled.

Furthermore, RBL tasks have several implications within clinical psychology since RBL is commonly used in word-learning contexts for children with learning disabilities. For instance, the review into RBL by Gordon (2020) found modern empirical evidence shows RBL can enhance word learning for children with learning disorders with there being guidance for clinicians on how to effectively apply RBL for word learning. Gordan (2020)'s findings are important for our results since this study used a word-learning task to teach students Japanese symbols, suggesting our results have direct implications for children with language disorders. This is further supported by additional studies, like Haebig et al. (2019), Leonard et al. (2019), Leonard et al. (2020) and Leonard and Deevy (2020). All finding RBL tasks help both typically-developing children and those with a language disorder learn novel word stimuli and experience long-term retention. Overall, a multitude of studies supports how our results can be used to implement real-world interventions to help children affected by developmental language disorders enhance their word learning, and given how language skills are highly predictable of a child's ability to read and success at school (Dickinson & Tabors, 2001; McCardle et al., 2001; Snow, Burns & Griffin, 2005; Snow et al., 1999; Stanovich et al., 1986; Storch & Whitehurst, 2001; Walker, Greenwood, Hart & Carta, 1994), this is an important problem needing an intervention. RBL tasks could be the intervention as showed in our results and those of other studies.

Our study had several limitations that need to be addressed in future research. Control groups are needed so researchers know if an intervention is working and these effects can be separated from the effects of other interventions (Pithon, 2013). Similar to how Randomised Controlled Trials (RCT) in clinical psychology research allow researchers to benefit from RCT being the most robust and empirical method for establishing whether a cause-and-effect relationships exists (Bhide et al., 2018). Although, our study did not use a control group so whilst our findings demonstrate our RBL task is helpful in participant learning and successful retrieval, this study cannot separate these effects from other interventions because this study cannot say if the successful retrieval was a result of our task or them doing a learning intervention regardless of the type used. Therefore, future research must use control groups to ensure the study's results are from the RBL intervention and not other variables.

Secondly, whilst our study found a decrease in Fmθ was related to learning and more success retrievals later on, this study did not investigate neuroelectric activity during the testing phase and since this study did not use a control group this study could not investigate cognitive effort in differentially difficult tasks. This would have given us more data to support our conclusions with and it would have made our study fit with additional literature. For example, Berry and Thompson (1978) found rabbits who showed higher theta activity learnt faster than rabbits with higher brain frequencies. Also, Mussel et al. (2016) found theta power reflects cognitive effort on tasks differing in difficulty and this is predictive of performance on these tasks. Together these studies demonstrate neuroelectric activity can be used to investigate motivational and effort mechanisms underpinning active learning tasks. Therefore, whilst our study did not look at these concepts, future research should investigate differences in neuroelectric differences between experimental and control groups to see whether such oscillatory differences can predict differences in performance to further add to the RBL literature.

Finally, whilst our study made used of a 1-week post-test element allowing us to understand the long-term impacts of our RBL intervention on participant performance, future research should make use of longer post-intervention periods to further understand the long-term effects of RBL. Since currently, this study can only say with empirical evidence, RBL is effective for one week following the intervention. Anything later this guessing. Also, this is a larger criticism of the RBL literature because a plethora of studies only use one-week post-intervention posts, like Agarwal et al. (2008), Karpicke and Grimaldi (2012) and Roediger and Butler (2011). Therefore, this limitation needs to be addressed in the literature because currently the longer term effects of RBL are unknown. Also, it is arguable the work of Sheffield and Hudson (2006), Memon et al. (1997) and Hudson (1990) nullifies this limitation because research shows improved retrieval of novel events and improved memory 8- and 12-weeks after learning. Yet RBL tasks were not used making the results difficult to compare and the research sample was 18-months old infants, pre-schoolers and elementary pupils, not adults. Hence, this limitation remains. Overall, future research should use different experimental groups with different post-intervention time periods, allowing researchers to learn if there is a limit or optimal gap between training and testing.

In conclusion, this study provides evidence

that a RBL task is useful in learning and this study explores several behavioural and neurological mechanisms for this efficacy. Mainly meta-learning or Transfer Effect were responsible, because this effect promotes successful retrieval by applying learning across similar contexts requiring less effort to learn. This is consistent with our results and Transfer Effect is widely supported in the literature as an underlying principle of learning (Pan & Rickard, 2018). These findings have valuable implications for RBL theories, like Transfer Appropriate Processing theory and Long-term Potentiation, because this is the first time neuroevidence on Transfer Effects has been conducted, directing future research towards using control groups, longitudinal methodology and investigating neural oscillations during the testing phase. Also, our results can be practically applied in clinical and educational settings where using active learning procedures to boost learning and performance is on the rise (Wirth & Perkins, 2008).

References

Abbott, E. E. (1909). On the analysis of the factor of recall in the learning process. *The Psychological Review: Monograph Supplements*, *11*(1), 159–177. https://doi.org/10.1037/h0093018

Agarwal, P. K., Karpicke, J. D., Kang, S. H., Roediger III, H. L., & McDermott, K. B. (2008). Examining the testing effect with open-and closed-book tests. *Applied Cognitive Psychology: The Official Journal of the Society for Applied Research in Memory and Cognition*, *22*(7), 861-876.

Anderson, J. R. (1996). ACT: A simple theory of complex cognition. American Psychologist, 51, 355–365. http://dx.doi.org/10.1037/0003- 066X.51.4.355

Ayres, P. L. (1993). Why Goal-Free Problems Can Facilitate Learning. *Contemporary Educational Psychology*, *18*(3), 376–381. https://doi.org/10.1006/ceps.1993.1027

Barnett, S. M., & Ceci, S. J. (2002). When and where do we apply what we learn?: A taxonomy for far transfer. *Psychological Bulletin*, *128*(4), 612–637. https://doi.org/10.1037/0033-2909.128.4.612

Berry, S. D., & Thompson, R. F. (1978). Prediction of learning rate from the hippocampal electroencephalogram. *Science*, *200*(4347), 1298-1300.

Bhide, A., Shah, P. S., & Acharya, G. (2018). A simplified guide to randomized controlled trials. *Acta Obstetricia Et Gynecologica Scandinavica*, *97*(4), 380–387. https://doi.org/10.1111/aogs.13309

Bjork, R. A. (1994). Memory and metamemory considerations in the training of human beings. In *Metacognition: Knowing about knowing.* (pp. 185–205). https://books.google.com/books?hl=en&lr=&id=Ci

0TDgAAQBAJ&oi=fnd&pg=PA185&ots=qG4y4uPvYs&sig=dDuK6kAtBmrkeOe5AsfI3nmK3aM

Bliss, T. V., & Collingridge, G. L. (1993). A synaptic model of memory: long-term potentiation in the hippocampus. *Nature, 361*(6407), 31-39.

Bobis, J., Sweller, J., & Cooper, M. (1994). Demands imposed on primary-school students by geometric models. *Contemporary Educational Psychology, 19*(1), 108–117. https://doi.org/10.1006/ceps.1994.1010

Buchin, Z. L., & Mulligan, N. W. (2023). Retrieval-based learning and prior knowledge. *Journal of Educational Psychology, 115*(1), 22.

Carpenter, S. K. (2011). Semantic information activated during retrieval contributes to later retention: Support for the mediator effectiveness hypothesis of the testing effect. *Journal of Experimental Psychology: Learning, Memory, and Cognition, 37*(6), 1547–1552. https://doi.org/10.1037/a0024140

Carpenter, S. K., & DeLosh, E. L. (2006). Impoverished cue support enhances subsequent retention: Support for the elaborative retrieval explanation of the testing effect. *Memory and Cognition, 34*(2), 268–276. https://doi.org/10.3758/BF03193405

Carpenter, S. K., Pashler, H., & Cepeda, N. J. (2009). Using tests to enhance 8th grade students' retention of US history facts. *Applied Cognitive Psychology: The Official Journal of the Society for Applied Research in Memory and Cognition, 23*(6), 760-771.

Chan, J. C. (2009). When does retrieval induce forgetting and when does it induce facilitation? Implications for retrieval inhibition, testing effect, and text processing. *Journal of Memory and Language, 61*(2),

153-170.

Chan, J. C. K., McDermott, K. B., & Roediger, H. L. III. (2006). Retrieval-induced facilitation: Initially nontested material can benefit from prior testing of related material. *Journal of Experimental Psychology: General, 135*(4), 553–571. https://doi.org/10.1037/0096-3445.135.4.553

Chi, Glaser, & Rees. (1982). Expertise in problem solving. In R. Sternberg (Ed.), *Advances in the Psychology of Human Intelligence* (pp. 7–75). Erlbaum, Hillsdale.

Coane, J. H. (2013). Retrieval practice and elaborative encoding benefit memory in younger and older adults. *Journal of Applied Research in Memory and Cognition, 2*(2), 95-100.

Collins, A. M., & Loftus, E. F. (1975). A spreading-activation theory of semantic processing. Psychological Review, 82, 407– 428. http://dx.doi.org/10.1037/0033-295X.82.6.407

Cooke, S. F., & Bliss, T. V. (2006). Plasticity in the human central nervous system. *Brain, 129*(7), 1659-1673.

Cranney, J., Ahn, M., McKinnon, R., Morris, S., & Watts, K. (2009). The testing effect, collaborative learning, and retrieval-induced facilitation in a classroom setting. *European Journal of Cognitive Psychology, 21*(6), 919-940.

Dickinson, D. K., & Tabors, P. O. (2001). *Beginning literacy with language: Young children learning at home and school.* Paul H Brookes Publishing.

Doppelmayr, M., Finkenzeller, T., & Sauseng, P. (2008). Frontal midline theta in the pre-shot phase of rifle shooting: differences between experts and novices. *Neuropsychologia*, *46*(5), 1463-1467.

Dunst, B., Benedek, M., Jauk, E., Bergner, S., Koschutnig, K., Sommer, M., ... & Neubauer, A. C. (2014). Neural efficiency as a function of task demands. *Intelligence*, *42*, 22-30.

Eschmann, K. C., Bader, R., & Mecklinger, A. (2018). Topographical differences of frontal-midline theta activity reflect functional differences in cognitive control abilities. Brain and cognition, 123, 57-64.

Fazio, L. K., & Marsh, E. J. (2019). Retrieval-based learning in children. *Current Directions in Psychological Science*, *28*(2), 111-116.

Friedman, R. B., Sullivan, K. L., Snider, S. F., Luta, G., & Jones, K. T. (2017). Leveraging the test effect to improve maintenance of the gains achieved through cognitive rehabilitation. *Neuropsychology*, *31*(2), 220.

Gates, A. I. (1917). Recitation as a factor in memorizing. *Archives of Psychology*, *6*(40). https://archive.org/stream/recitationasafa00gategoog?ref=ol#page/n22/mode/2up

Gevins, A., Smith, M. E., McEvoy, L., & Yu, D. (1997). High-resolution EEG mapping of cortical activation related to working memory: effects of task difficulty, type of processing, and practice. *Cerebral cortex (New York, NY: 1991)*, *7*(4), 374-385.

Gordon, K. R. (2020). The advantages of retrieval-based and spaced practice: Implications for word learning in clinical and educational contexts. *Language, Speech, and Hearing Services in Schools*, *51*(4), 955-965.

Haebig, E., Leonard, L. B., Deevy, P., Karpicke, J., Christ, S. L., Usler, E., ... & Weber, C. (2019).

Retrieval-based word learning in young typically developing children and children with development language disorder II: A comparison of retrieval schedules. *Journal of Speech, Language, and Hearing Research*, 62(4), 944-964.

Haebig, E., Leonard, L. B., Deevy, P., Schumaker, J., Karpicke, J. D., & Weber, C. (2021). The neural underpinnings of processing newly taught semantic information: The role of retrieval practice. *Journal of Speech, Language, and Hearing Research*, 64(8), 3195-3211.

Hsieh, L. T., & Ranganath, C. (2014). Frontal midline theta oscillations during working memory maintenance and episodic encoding and retrieval. Neuroimage, 85, 721-729.

Hudson, J. A. (1990). Constructive processing in children's event memory. Developmental Psychology, 26, 180–187.

Ishii, R., Canuet, L., Ishihara, T., Aoki, Y., Ikeda, S., Hata, M., ... & Takeda, M. (2014). Frontal midline theta rhythm and gamma power changes during focused attention on mental calculation: an MEG beamformer analysis. *Frontiers in human neuroscience, 8*, 406.

Jutras, M. J., & Buffalo, E. A. (2014). Oscillatory correlates of memory in non-human primates. Neuroimage, 85, 694-701.

Karpicke, J. D., & Grimaldi, P. J. (2012). Retrieval-based learning: A perspective for enhancing meaningful learning. *Educational Psychology Review*, 24(3), 401-418.

Khader, P. H., Jost, K., Ranganath, C., & Rösler, F. (2010). Theta and alpha oscillations during working-memory maintenance predict successful long-term memory encoding. Neuroscience letters, 468(3), 339-343.

Klimesch, W., & Doppelmayr, M. (1996). encoding of new. Neuroreport, 7, 1235-1240.

Klimesch, W., Schimke, H. A. N. N. E. S., & Pfurtscheller, G. (1993). Alpha frequency, cognitive load and memory performance. Brain topography, 5(3), 241-251.

Kornell, N., Bjork, R. A., & Garcia, M. A. (2011). Why tests appear to prevent forgetting: A distribution-based bifurcation model. *Journal of Memory and Language*, 65(2), 85–97. https://doi.org/10.1016/j.jml.2011.04.002

Leonard, L. B., & Deevy, P. (2020). Retrieval practice and word learning in children with specific language impairment and their typically developing peers. *Journal of Speech, Language, and Hearing Research*, 63(10), 3252-3262.

Leonard, L. B., Deevy, P., Karpicke, J. D., Christ, S. L., & Kueser, J. B. (2020). After initial retrieval practice, more retrieval produces better retention than more study in the word learning of children with developmental language disorder. *Journal of Speech, Language, and Hearing Research*, 63(8), 2763-2776.

Leonard, L. B., Karpicke, J., Deevy, P., Weber, C., Christ, S., Haebig, E., ... & Krok, W. (2019). Retrieval-based word learning in young typically developing children and children with developmental language disorder I: The benefits of repeated retrieval. *Journal of Speech, Language, and Hearing Research*, 62(4), 932-943.

Lipowski, S. L., Pyc, M. A., Dunlosky, J., & Rawson, K. A. (2014). Establishing and explaining the testing effect in free recall for young children. *Developmental Psychology*, *50*(4), 994.

McCardle, P., Scarborough, H. S., & Catts, H. W. (2001). Predicting, explaining, and preventing children's reading difficulties. *Learning disabilities research & practice*, *16*(4), 230-239.

McDaniel, M. A. (2007). Transfer: Rediscovering a central concept. In H. L. Roediger, Y. Dudai, & S. M. Fitzpatrick (Eds.), Science of memory: Concepts. New York, NY: Oxford University Press.

Memon, A., Wark, L., Bull, R., & Koehnken, G. (1997). Isolating the effects of the cognitive interview techniques. British Journal of Psychology, 88, 179–197. doi:10.1111/j.2044-8295.1997.tb02629.x

Murdock, B. B., & Dufty, P. O. (1972). Strength theory and recognition memory. *Journal of Experimental Psychology*. https://doi.org/10.1037/h0032795

Mussel, P., Ulrich, N., Allen, J. J., Osinsky, R., & Hewig, J. (2016). Patterns of theta oscillation reflect the neural basis of individual differences in epistemic motivation. *Scientific reports*, *6*(1), 1-10.

Neubauer, A. C., & Fink, A. (2009). Intelligence and neural efficiency. *Neuroscience & Biobehavioral Reviews*, *33*(7), 1004-1023.

Nguyen, P., Nguyen, T. A., & Zeng, Y. (2018). Empirical approaches to quantifying effort, fatigue and concentration in the conceptual design process. *Research in Engineering Design*, *29*(3), 393-409.

Norman, D. A., & Wickelgren, W. A. (1969). Strength theory of decision rules and latency in retrieval from short-term memory. *Journal of Mathematical Psychology*. https://doi.org/10.1016/0022-2496(69)90002-9

Norman, D. A., & Wickelgren, W. A. (1969). Strength theory of decision rules and latency in retrieval from short-term memory. *Journal of Mathematical Psychology.* https://doi.org/10.1016/0022-2496(69)90002-9

Owen, E., & Sweller, J. (1985). What Do Students Learn While Solving Mathematics Problems? *Journal of Educational Psychology,* 77(3), 272–284. https://doi.org/10.1037/0022-0663.77.3.272

Ozubko, J. (2011). Is Free Recall Actually Superior to Cued Recall? Introducing the Recognized Recall Procedure to Examine the Costs and Benefits of Cueing. *A Thesis Presented to the University of Waterloo.*

Pan, S. C., & Rickard, T. C. (2018). Transfer of test-enhanced learning: Meta-analytic review and synthesis. *Psychological bulletin, 144*(7), 710.

Pithon, M. M. (2013). Importance of the control group in scientific research. Dental Press Journal of Orthodontics, 18(6), 13-14.

Pyc, M. A., & Rawson, K. A. (2009). Testing the retrieval effort hypothesis: Does greater difficulty correctly recalling information lead to higher levels of memory? *Journal of Memory and Language, 60*(4), 437–447. https://doi.org/10.1016/j.jml.2009.01.004

Pyke, W., Vostanis, A., & Javadi, A. H. (2021). Electrical Brain Stimulation During a Retrieval-Based Learning Task Can Impair Long-Term Memory. *Journal of Cognitive Enhancement, 5*(2), 218-232.

Raaijmakers, J. G., & Shiffrin, R. M. (1981).

Search of associative memory. Psychological Review, 88, 93–134. http://dx.doi.org/10.1037/0033-295X.88.2.93

Reber, P. J., & Kotovsky, K. (1997). Implicit learning in problem solving: The role of working memory capacity. *Journal of Experimental Psychology: General, 126*(2), 178.

Riddle, J., Scimeca, J. M., Cellier, D., Dhanani, S., & D'Esposito, M. (2020). Causal evidence for a role of theta and alpha oscillations in the control of working memory. Current Biology, 30(9), 1748-1754.

Roediger III, H. L., & Butler, A. C. (2011). The critical role of retrieval practice in long-term retention. *Trends in cognitive sciences, 15*(1), 20-27.

Roediger III, H. L., & Karpicke, J. D. (2006). Test-enhanced learning: Taking memory tests improves long-term retention. *Psychological science, 17*(3), 249-255.

Sanders, L. L. O., Ponte, R. P., Viana, A. B., Peixoto, A. A., Kubrusly, M., & Leitão, A. M. F. (2019). Retrieval-Based Learning in Neuroanatomy Classes. *Revista Brasileira de Educação Médica, 43*, 92-98.

Schüler, A., Scheiter, K., & van Genuchten, E. (2011). The role of working memory in multimedia instruction: Is working memory working during learning from text and pictures?. *Educational Psychology Review, 23*(3), 389-411.

Sheffield, E. G., & Hudson, J. A. (2006). You must remember this: Effects of video and photograph reminders on 18-month-olds' event memory. Journal of Cognition and Development, 7, 73–93. doi:10.1207/s15327647jcd0701_4

Smith, M. A., Roediger III, H. L., & Karpicke, J. D. (2013). Covert retrieval practice benefits retention as much as overt retrieval practice. *Journal of Experimental Psychology: Learning, Memory, and Cognition, 39*(6), 1712.

Snow, C. E., Griffin, P. E., & Burns, M. (2005). *Knowledge to support the teaching of reading: Preparing teachers for a changing world.* Jossey-Bass.

Snow, C., Burns, M. S., & Griffin, P. (1999). *Language and literacy environments in preschools.*

Spitzer, H. F. (1939). Studies in retention. *Journal of Educational Psychology, 30*(9), 641–656. https://doi.org/10.1037/h0063404

Stanovich, K. E., Nathan, R. G., & Vala-Rossi, M. (1986). Developmental changes in the cognitive correlates of reading ability and the developmental lag hypothesis. *Reading research quarterly*, 267-283.

Storch, S. A., & Whitehurst, G. J. (2001). The role of family and home in the literacy development of children from low-income backgrounds. *New directions for child and adolescent development, 2001*(92), 53-72.

Sweller, J. (1988). Cognitive Load During Problem Solving: Effects on Learning. *Cognitive Science, 12*(2), 257–285. https://doi.org/10.1207/s15516709cog1202_4

Sweller, J., Van Merrienboer, J. J. G., & Paas, F. G. W. C. (1998). Cognitive Architecture and Instructional Design. *Educational Psychology Review, 10*(3), 251–296. https://doi.org/10.1023/A:1022193728205

Sya'ban, S. N., Wazir, A., & Horneffer, P. Retrieval-Based Learning Strategies in Medical Education

Thompson, R. F. (2005). In search of memory traces. *Annu. Rev. Psychol., 56*, 1-23.

Vollmeyer, R., Burns, B. D., & Holyoak, K. J. (1996). The Impact of Goal Specificity on Strategy Use and the Acquisition of Problem Structure. *Cognitive Science*, *20*(1), 75–100. https://doi.org/10.1207/s15516709cog2001_3

Walker, D., Greenwood, C., Hart, B., & Carta, J. (1994). Prediction of school outcomes based on early language production and socioeconomic factors. *Child development*, *65*(2), 606-621.

Wu, J., Srinivasan, R., Burke Quinlan, E., Solodkin, A., Small, S. L., & Cramer, S. C. (2016). Utility of EEG measures of brain function in patients with acute stroke. *Journal of neurophysiology*, *115*(5), 2399-2405.

Appendix A

A List of Our Stimuli
Bear - Kuma
Blue - Ao
Body - Karada
Bone - Hone
Book - Hon
Branch - Eda
Broom - Houki
Cheek - Hoho
Chopsticks - Hashi
Cliff - Gake
Cloud - Kumo
Colour - Iro
Crab -Kani
Dog - Inu
Dove - Hato
Face - Kao
Father - Chichi
Field - Hatake
Fist - Kobushi
Flower - Hana
Fountain - Izumi
Fox - Kitsune
Frog - Kaeru
Hair - Kami
Head - Atama
House - Ie
Key - Kagi
Leaf - Ha
Lung - Hai
Mirror - Kagami
Mother - Haha

Mouth - Kuchi
Nose - Hana
Oil - Abura
Owl - Fukurou
Pig - Buta
Pond - Ike
Rain - Ame
Red - Aka
Sheep - Hitsuji
Star - Hoshi
Station - Eki
Stomach - i
Stone - Ishi
Strawberry - Ichigo
Tree - Ki
Wall - Kabe
Wind - Kaze

https://www.subscribepage.com/psychologyboxset

CHECK OUT THE PSYCHOLOGY WORLD PODCAST FOR MORE PSYCHOLOGY INFORMATION! AVAILABLE ON ALL MAJOR PODCAST APPS.

About the author:

Connor Whiteley is the author of over 60 books in the sci-fi fantasy, nonfiction psychology and books for writer's genre and he is a Human Branding Speaker and Consultant.

He is a passionate warhammer 40,000 reader, psychology student and author.

Who narrates his own audiobooks and he hosts The Psychology World Podcast.

All whilst studying Psychology at the University of Kent, England.

Also, he was a former Explorer Scout where he gave a speech to the Maltese President in August 2018 and he attended Prince Charles' 70th Birthday Party at Buckingham Palace in May 2018.

Plus, he is a self-confessed coffee lover!

All books in 'An Introductory Series':
Careers In Psychology
Psychology of Suicide
Dementia Psychology
Clinical Psychology Reflections Volume 4
Forensic Psychology of Terrorism And Hostage-Taking
Forensic Psychology of False Allegations
Year In Psychology
CBT For Anxiety
CBT For Depression
Applied Psychology
BIOLOGICAL PSYCHOLOGY 3RD EDITION
COGNITIVE PSYCHOLOGY THIRD EDITION
SOCIAL PSYCHOLOGY- 3RD EDITION
ABNORMAL PSYCHOLOGY 3RD EDITION
PSYCHOLOGY OF RELATIONSHIPS- 3RD EDITION
DEVELOPMENTAL PSYCHOLOGY 3RD EDITION
HEALTH PSYCHOLOGY
RESEARCH IN PSYCHOLOGY
A GUIDE TO MENTAL HEALTH AND TREATMENT AROUND THE WORLD-

A GLOBAL LOOK AT DEPRESSION
FORENSIC PSYCHOLOGY
THE FORENSIC PSYCHOLOGY OF THEFT, BURGLARY AND OTHER CRIMES AGAINST PROPERTY
CRIMINAL PROFILING: A FORENSIC PSYCHOLOGY GUIDE TO FBI PROFILING AND GEOGRAPHICAL AND STATISTICAL PROFILING.
CLINICAL PSYCHOLOGY
FORMULATION IN PSYCHOTHERAPY
PERSONALITY PSYCHOLOGY AND INDIVIDUAL DIFFERENCES
CLINICAL PSYCHOLOGY REFLECTIONS VOLUME 1
CLINICAL PSYCHOLOGY REFLECTIONS VOLUME 2
Clinical Psychology Reflections Volume 3
CULT PSYCHOLOGY
Police Psychology

A Psychology Student's Guide To University
How Does University Work?
A Student's Guide To University And Learning
University Mental Health and Mindset

Other books by Connor Whiteley:

Bettie English Private Eye Series

A Very Private Woman
The Russian Case
A Very Urgent Matter
A Case Most Personal
Trains, Scots and Private Eyes
The Federation Protects
Cops, Robbers and Private Eyes
Just Ask Bettie English
An Inheritance To Die For
The Death of Graham Adams
Bearing Witness
The Twelve
The Wrong Body
The Assassination Of Bettie English

Lord of War Origin Trilogy:

Not Scared Of The Dark
Madness
Burn Them All

The Fireheart Fantasy Series

Heart of Fire
Heart of Lies
Heart of Prophecy
Heart of Bones

Heart of Fate

City of Assassins (Urban Fantasy)
City of Death
City of Marytrs
City of Pleasure
City of Power

Agents of The Emperor
Return of The Ancient Ones
Vigilance
Angels of Fire
Kingmaker
The Eight
The Lost Generation
Hunt
Emperor's Council
Speaker of Treachery
Birth Of The Empire
Terraforma

The Rising Augusta Fantasy Adventure Series
Rise To Power
Rising Walls
Rising Force
Rising Realm

Lord Of War Trilogy (Agents of The Emperor)
Not Scared Of The Dark
Madness
Burn It All Down

Gay Romance Novellas
Breaking, Nursing, Repairing A Broken Heart
Jacob And Daniel
Fallen For A Lie
Spying And Weddings

Miscellaneous:
RETURN
FREEDOM
SALVATION
Reflection of Mount Flame
The Masked One
The Great Deer
English Independence

OTHER SHORT STORIES BY CONNOR WHITELEY

Mystery Short Story Collections

Criminally Good Stories Volume 1: 20 Detective Mystery Short Stories
Criminally Good Stories Volume 2: 20 Private Investigator Short Stories
Criminally Good Stories Volume 3: 20 Crime Fiction Short Stories
Criminally Good Stories Volume 4: 20 Science Fiction and Fantasy Mystery Short Stories
Criminally Good Stories Volume 5: 20 Romantic Suspense Short Stories

Mystery Short Stories:

Protecting The Woman She Hated
Finding A Royal Friend
Our Woman In Paris
Corrupt Driving
A Prime Assassination
Jubilee Thief
Jubilee, Terror, Celebrations
Negative Jubilation
Ghostly Jubilation
Killing For Womenkind
A Snowy Death

Miracle Of Death
A Spy In Rome
The 12:30 To St Pancreas
A Country In Trouble
A Smokey Way To Go
A Spicy Way To GO
A Marketing Way To Go
A Missing Way To Go
A Showering Way To Go
Poison In The Candy Cane
Kendra Detective Mystery Collection Volume 1
Kendra Detective Mystery Collection Volume 2
Mystery Short Story Collection Volume 1
Mystery Short Story Collection Volume 2
Criminal Performance
Candy Detectives
Key To Birth In The Past

<u>Science Fiction Short Stories:</u>
Their Brave New World
Gummy Bear Detective
The Candy Detective
What Candies Fear
The Blurred Image
Shattered Legions

The First Rememberer
Life of A Rememberer
System of Wonder
Lifesaver
Remarkable Way She Died
The Interrogation of Annabella Stormic
Blade of The Emperor
Arbiter's Truth
Computation of Battle
Old One's Wrath
Puppets and Masters
Ship of Plague
Interrogation
Edge of Failure

<u>Fantasy Short Stories:</u>
City of Snow
City of Light
City of Vengeance
Dragons, Goats and Kingdom
Smog The Pathetic Dragon
Don't Go In The Shed
The Tomato Saver
The Remarkable Way She Died
Dragon Coins
Dragon Tea
Dragon Rider

www.ingramcontent.com/pod-product-compliance
Lightning Source LLC
LaVergne TN
LVHW011845060526
838200LV00054B/4177